# YORKSH
## PLACE NAMES

*Robert Gambles*

1995

# Dalesman Publishing Company

Stable Courtyard, Broughton Hall,
Skipton, North Yorkshire BD23 3AE


**First published 1995**


© Robert Gambles 1995

Cover photograph Burnsall in Wharfedale by John Morrison
Drawings by Den Oldroyd


A British Library Cataloguing in Publication record
is available for this book

**ISBN 185568 094 7**


Printed by Hubbards

# CONTENTS

Preface    4

Introduction    5

Note on the languages    9

Swaledale (with Arkengarthdale)    12

Wensleydale (with Bishopdale and Coverdale)    22

Dentdale (with Garsdale)    36

Ribblesdale (with Kingsdale)    46

Airedale (with Malhamdale)    57

Wharfedale (with Littondale and Langstrothdale)    63

Upper Nidderdale    74

Glossary    83

Index    89

Bibliography    95

# PREFACE

This companion volume to the author's Lake District Place-names retains the essential form of its predecessor and has the same aim - to explain the origin and meaning of place-names in a manner which combines simplicity with the minimum of linguistic information necessary for an intelligent understanding of each name. Place-names have a special fascination for those who live in an area so rich in its heritage as the Yorkshire Dales and also for those who come to visit and find these northern names so very different from those in other parts of the country. Dull would he be of soul who could pass incuriously by such names as Crackpot, Snaizeholme, Trollers Gill and Yockenthwaite, while many might regret the passing of beavers from Barben Beck, wolves from Uldale and cloudberries from Knoutberry Haw. To understand the origin of place-names can be to discover the key to a better appreciation of the countryside our English and Norse ancestors knew so well 1,000 years ago.

I am indebted to the work of those scholars who have devoted their expert knowledge of linguistics to the study of northern place-names. Any student of this subject must acknowledge a debt to the English Place-name Society whose volumes are the starting point of any enquiry in this field. The publications which cover the Yorkshire Dales are the volume on the Place-names of the North Riding and Parts 6 and 7 of the Place-names of the West Riding (Cambridge University Press).

I wish also to acknowledge with gratitude the patient guidance of Professor A. D. Mills of Liverpool University who gently steered me away from some of the pitfalls which lie in wait for any unwary adventurer in pursuit of the origin of place-names. Any errors are my own.

ROBERT GAMBLES

# INTRODUCTION

Place-names were formed from words once commonly used in everyday speech, words which described one particular spot and distinguished it unmistakably from other places in the immediate neighbourhood. Such a description might have been no more than a simple identification of the man or family who lived there - thus, Yockenthwaite was 'the clearing where Eoghan lived - or it might have referred to some natural feature nearby - such as at Beckermonds, 'the place where the streams meet' - or, perhaps, to some well-known local superstition as at Grimwith - 'the wood haunted by a ghost'. Whatever the description it would leave no doubt within a small community of the exact location of the place referred to.

All place-names were therefore used in spoken form long before they first appeared in written records, and transmission in this way, perhaps for many generations, resulted in subtle changes which now present difficult problems for the place-name scholar. The early written versions of a place-name are usually the most helpful guide to its original meaning, and yet these may often be no more than semi-phonetic spellings in a language alien to the first recorder and now no longer in use. It is also important to bear in mind that the modern form of any place-name could be the result of recent standardised spelling usages and so might prove an unreliable guide to the original name.

The study of place-names is, therefore, most properly the province of the scholar in linguistic studies and demands a detailed understanding of the structure and development of several now obsolete languages. For the non-specialist this is inevitably dangerous territory, and for the 'happy guesser' it is a veritable minefield. Even so, place-names hold a special fascination for many people and an intelligent understanding of their structure and origin can add a new dimension to the appreciation and enjoyment of our historical heritage.

For all of us, specialist or not, place-names can be an intriguing source of information about our remote ancestors who first gave names to our farms, fields, rivers, hills and valleys, towns and villages. They can also tell us of the birds and animals and the plants and flowers which the early settlers found in these places; they reveal something of their folklore, religious beliefs, land use, local customs, trade routes and, of course, the language they spoke. The first settlers in the Yorkshire Dales were probably the prehistoric folk who lived by Semer Water or in Victoria Cave and left behind their flint axes and arrow-heads, stone carvings and fragments of pottery. We know nothing of their language and it is unlikely that any place-names are derived from that period. In the centuries before the arrival of the Romans and for the 400 years of the Roman occupation the Dales (and almost the whole of the north) were the territory of the Brigantes, the powerful Celtic tribe who were so troublesome to the Roman governors and whose field enclosures, hill forts and upland settlements may still be traced, notably near Malham and Penhill and at Maiden Castle. The Celtic language was common to Iron Age tribes in many parts of Europe and it has survived in regional variations such as Breton, Gaelic, Cornish and Welsh. A tentative reconstruction of many words has therefore been possible and we know that many of the names of our rivers and hills are Celtic in origin - names such as Penyghent, Penhill, Ure, Wharfe and Nidd - but otherwise the Celtic names were swept into oblivion with the arrival of the Anglo-Saxon colonisers in the 7th and 8th centuries.

The Roman legions left little mark on the place-names of this remote part of their vast empire; the names of their once bustling camps and townships have been erased almost completely. Who in the Yorkshire Dales would now enquire the way to Virosidium or Olicana?

The Celtic tribes often lived in uneasy co-existence with the Roman conquerors whom they supplied with food, material goods and slave labour, but the Anglo-Saxons were settlers and farmers who required none of these things and relentlessly drove out the Celts from the land they coveted. The name 'Walden' tells the story of a people confined to a small remote valley, 'aliens' in their own country.

As the Anglo-Saxons moved into the fertile valleys they gave 'English' names to the fields they created and to the natural features around them. Words such as 'ham' (homestead), 'tun' (farmstead), 'leah' (woodland clearing), 'denu' (valley) and 'stan' (stone) and many more became common and have come down to us in such names as Coverham, Middleham, Horton, Litton, Cautley, Healaugh, Hebden, Cogden, Kidstones and Stainforth.

In the early 10th century a new and overwhelming wave of settlers began to pour into the Dales. These were the Norsemen, mainly Norwegians, who had already established themselves in West Scotland, Ireland and North West

# Area covered by this book

Arkengarthdale

Birkdale

Swaledale

Garsdale

Widdale

Wensleydale

Bishopdale

Dentdale

Coverdale

Kingsdale

Langstrothdale

Ribblesdale

Littondale

Nidderdale

Airedale

Wharfedale

*Border denotes edge of Yorkshire Dales National Park*

England. They were not the plundering, axe-wielding Viking warriors from whose fury a special Litany asked for God's protection, but simple farming families seeking a new life and new lands to settle on. They preferred to live in scattered farmsteads, preferably in the uplands or valley heads, and so they did not compete with the English who preferred the more congenial lowlands and liked to live in small communities or hamlets. Norse influence on the place-names of the Dales was profound: some two-thirds of all the names here have a Norwegian derivation while the dialect speech of the area still retains many words and phrases of Norse origin. Swaledale was the last place in England where the Norse language was spoken but by the mid-13th century this gave way to a blend of language which was to form part of the 'English' which became Europe's most versatile language. Many of these Norsemen have left us their names in the place-names they created often attached to the upland farms they owned - seters - or to the clearings they so arduously made in the forest - thwaites. Norse words abound throughout the Dales - by, gill, beck, fell, scale and lathe will be met at every turn.

Less than 200 years later the Norman Conquest shattered the Anglo-Norse kingdom of England. Norman barons carved up the land into great estates and imposed unwelcome taxes and restrictions on the hitherto independent farmers. Roger of Poitou was succeeded by the Scropes, the Nevilles and the Cliffords in dominance over the Dales, but these were just a handful of overlords not a new race of colonisers and their impact on the language of their conquered people was negligible. Such French influence as there was came from those other great post-Conquest landowners - the monastic foundations. The abbeys of Furness, Fountains, Jervaulx and Sawley as well as Bolton Priory and several smaller houses all held extensive estates in the Dales where they established their sheep-runs, cereal, stock and dairy farms, horse studs and granges. Links with these may be found in names such as Fountains Fell, Abbotside, Prior's Rake and Grange.

The town of Richmond is perhaps the only place of importance which lost its earlier name - Hindrelac - to be replaced by the French 'Richemont'.

Few place-names have been added in more recent times. The lead miners brought the name 'hush' to Swaledale and Arkengarthdale as in Turf Moor Hush and Bunton Hush; the threats from Scottish raiders and other invaders introduced the many 'beacons' on the hills as at Beamsley and on Shunner Fell; 19th century patriotism gave us Victoria Cave while various local families and now unknown individuals gave their names to Yorke's Folly, Parcevall Hall, Ghaistrill's Strid, Simpson's Pot and Janet's Foss.

These post-Norman Conquest names form only a tiny proportion of all the place-names to be found in the Yorkshire Dales. By far the great majority - perhaps more than 95% - owe their origin to the humble folk who first cleared the forest, drained the swamps and 'stubbed the waste' to create their homesteads just over 1,000 years ago.

# NOTE ON THE LANGUAGES

Scholars who study place-names have a particular expertise in the languages of the different peoples who came to settle in the various parts of Britain: the Britons and Celts whose language was the forerunner of Welsh; the Angles and Saxons whose language we know as Old English; the Norsemen who spoke Old Norse, the ancestor of modern Icelandic, Danish and Norwegian; and the Norman-French who had a marginal influence on the development of the English language in the Middle ages.

For the laymen these erudite linguistic studies are daunting and can even be a barrier to an understanding of the meaning of place-names. The presentation of the place-name analysis in this guide simplifies these linguistic problems in order to facilitate this understanding but in a form which is not inconsistent with academic accuracy.

The following points should be noted:

i.     Old English and Old Norse employed certain letters which are no longer in use: The letters ð and þ which in these languages represent the sound 'th' as in 'thin' and 'thus' are represented in the text by their modern equivalent 'th' - e.g. the common Norse word 'þ veit' is shown as 'thveit'.

The letter ǫ in Old Norse indicates a particular 'o' sound. This is not shown in any distinctive way other than by the letter 'o'.

The letter æ in both early languages represents a particular 'a' sound.

ii.     The signs - and ' over certain vowels indicate a long sound in Old English and Old Norse respectively and are important guides to later linguistic development but they have been omitted in the text here.

iii.     Old English uses the letter 'c' where Old Norse uses the letter 'k'; as for example in OE cirice which in ON becomes kirkja.

iv.     Old English uses 'c', and 'sc' where Modern English usually uses 'ch' and 'sh' as, for example, OE cirice = church; OE sceap = sheep.

The following abbreviations have been used to indicate the language of origin of the place-name elements:

Br.  Words of British or Celtic origin.
Wel.  Words derived from Old Welsh.
OE.  Old English (5th - 11th centuries).
ON.  Old Norse.
ODan. Old Danish.
OFr.  Old French.
ME.  Middle English (12th - 15th centuries).
Dial.  Words used in North Country dialects.

## NOTE ON SÆTR

This Old Norse word is variously translated as 'shieling', 'mountain hut', 'summer pasture', 'upland pasture' and 'upland farm'. Its modern equivalent is the Norwegian word 'seter' and until recent years this was still an important feature of the pattern of agriculture in Norway. Sheep, cows and goats were driven to long-established upland pastures during the summer months to graze freely on the rich grass and herbage there. At the seter sites were log chalets which were the summer living quarters of the women and girls who moved up with the stock, tended them and produced butter and cheese from the milk. With the onset of late Autumn and the first snows the seter was closed down for the winter and the animals driven down to the main farm in the valley. This system of transhumance farming was common in upland regions throughout Europe, including the Yorkshire Dales and the Lake District where place-names which refer to 'seters' are quite numerous.

As no single word or phrase in English fully conveys the precise meaning of 'sætr' the modern Norwegian word 'seter' is given as a more satisfactory translation.

## PLAN OF THE BOOK

With the exception of Nidderdale all the Dales included in this guide fall within the boundary of the Yorkshire Dales National Park. A few towns of particular interest just outside the Park have also been included. It is self-evidently not possible in a short guide to include the name of every field, wood, barn and beck in so large an area and a disciplined selection has been necessary in order to produce the 600 place-names which appear in this book.

The names are listed in alphabetical order under the following sections:
i.     Swaledale (with Arkengarthdale).
ii.    Wensleydale (with Bishopdale and Coverdale).
iii.   Dentdale (with Garsdale).

iv.    Ribblesdale (with Kingsdale).

v.    Airdale (with Malhamdale).

vi.    Wharfedale (with Littondale and Langstrothdale).

vii.    Upper Nidderdale.

The most useful guide to the original meaning of a place-name is to be found in the first written versions of the name. These appear in a variety of sources: pre-Conquest Histories, Domesday Book, Charters and Account Books of the great Abbeys, State Documents, Estate Deeds, Parish Registers, Wills, old maps, local records, Court Proceedings and even on ancient gravestones. Where a place-name has a recorded early version this is given in the text; where no early written form is available but where the meaning of the name seems fairly clear or can  reasonably be deduced this is indicated by the name with an asterisk *.

The analysis of each name is given as follows:

i.    The modern name.

ii.    An early version or an asterisk *.

iii.    The linguistic analysis.

iv.    The meaning of the name.

v.    Where any place has features of special historical or natural interest these are referred to briefly immediately after the analysis.

To avoid frequent repetition in the text a glossary of all the linguistic elements which occur in the place-names in this book is given on Pages 83 to 88. The precise meaning of each element which goes to make up any name will be found here.

An Index of all the place-names in the book with their references appears at the end of the book.

## MAPS

The Ordnance Survey Maps which cover the Yorkshire Dales are:

O.S. Touring Map and Guide no. 6: The Yorkshire Dales (1" to 1 mile).

O.S. Outdoor Leisure Maps of the Yorkshire Dales: ($2^1/_2$" to 1 mile).

No. 2 The Western Area: (Ribblesdale, Kingsdale, Dentdale, Garsdale).

No. 10. The Southern Area: (Airedale, Malhamdale, Wharfedale).

No. 30. The Northern and Central Areas: (Swaledale, Wensleydale, and Upper Nidderdale).

# SWALEDALE
## WITH ARKENGARTHDALE AND BIRKDALE

Swaledale, near Muker

**Swaledale:** Sualua 730. Possibly derived from ON svirla/OE swillian = to swirl, although the precise derivation is uncertain: + ON dalr. The valley of the River Swale, the swirling, rushing river.

*IN THE 30 miles from its source on the bleak, sweeping moorland of Birkdale to the elegant and historic town of Richmond, the River Swale flows through a narrow, winding valley of austere beauty, bright with the sparkle of rivers, becks and waterfalls, fragrant with the hay and flowers of its famous meadows, warm with the colourful sandstone of its cottages, farms, walls and innumerable field barns; but also a valley surrounded by the haunting solitude of wild and empty hills, and touched with the melancholy of the decaying relics of human endeavour, the ruins, the spoilheaps, the scars of the leadmines which once brought a respite from poverty to those who could endure the savage labour involved. To the modern tourist this is now Herriot country, 'as seen on T.V.', a scenic joy, the home of the black-faced Swaledale sheep and the source of Swaledale cheese. To the masochists on the Pennine Way Swaledale offers perhaps the most appealing few miles of their journey.*

## Arkengarthdale:
Arkillesgarth 1199. ON personal name, Arkil + ON garthr + ON dalr. The valley where Arkil has his enclosure.

*FROM Reeth in Swaledale a narrow road goes north alongside the Arkle Beck passing through hamlets whose names declare their Norse origins and are fascinating in their strange outlandlishness: Booze, Whaw, Faggergill and Eskeleth. Here, too, is CB, the shortest place-name in the country. This is Arkengarthdale, the most northerly of the Dales, once busy with a lead-mining industry which has left behind it ruined buildings of many kinds and slowly healing scars in the landscape. A sense of poignant beauty pervades this valley.*

## Birkdale:
Birkdale 1301. ON birki + ON dalr. Birch tree valley.

*THERE are few birch trees in Birkdale now. This is a daunting landscape, wild and empty moorland, the domain of the Rough Fell sheep. The only road is the old Drove Road from Swaledale to Kirkby Stephen.*

**Aiskew:** Aichescou 1154. ON eik + skogr. The oak wood. The same name occurs near Dufton in Westmorland.

**Angram:** Angram 1195. OE anger (dative plural = angrum). By the pastures.

**Annaside:** *Probably ON personal name, Einarr + ON sætr. Einarr's seter.

**Applegarth:** * ON epli + ON garthr. The enclosure with an apple tree.

**Arkle Town:** Arkilton 1476. ON personal name, Arkil + ON tun. Arkil's farmstead.

**Aygill:** * ON a + ON gil. The river in a ravine.

**Beldon:** * ME bel + OE dun. Beacon hill.

**Bents:** * OE beonet. Bent grass, a coarse grass common in sheep pastures.

**Blakethwaite:** * The same name occurs near Orton in Westmorland and is recorded as Blakethwaite 1689. Probably OE blaec + ON thveit. Dark clearing.

**Booze:** Bowehous 1473. OE boga + OE/ON hus. The house on the curve (of the hill).

**Buttertubs:** * The origin of this name is obscure. It has been variously suggested that this was where tubs of butter were cooled on the way to market and that the potholes themselves bear a similarity to the shape of butter tubs. No linguistic derivation is available.

*These strange potholes are found near the roadside on the pass between Swaledale and Wensleydale north of Hawes. They are approximately 60 feet (20m) deep and have fluted sides from the action of the water draining off the surrounding peatbogs.*

**CB:** This the only place-name in Britain to consist of initial letters only. They belong to Charles Bathurst.

*Charles Bathurst was the grandson of John Bathurst, physician to Oliver Cromwell, who in 1656 bought the Manor of Arkengarthdale with a view to exploiting the local lead deposits. For the next 250 years the Bathurst family developed the lead mines nearby and created the hamlet named after Charles Bathurst (CB). The landscape was severely scarred by spoilheaps, adits, hushes and the ruins of mine buildings. Near CB stands an impressive hexagonal Powder House built in 1807 to store gunpowder. The CB Hotel is now the only other building of significance in the vicinity.*

**Cleasby:** Clesbi 1086 ODan personal name, Kless + ON by. Kless's farmstead. Kless is derived from ON kleiss meaning inarticulate, tongue-tied.

**Cogden:** Cockenden 14th c. OE cocc + OE denu. Woodcock valley.

**Copperthwaite:** Cowpertwaht 1566. ME coupare + ON thveit. Cooper's clearing. Cooper or Cowper may be a surname or, possibly, an occupation.

**Crackpot:** Crackpot 1298. ON kraka + ME potte. The crevice where crows nest. 'Pot' here indicates a limestone crevice rather than a pot-hole.

*Crackpot Hall is a good example of a small hill farm which could only survive when income was supplemented by work at the lead mines in the hills nearby. The farm was abandoned when the mines ceased to operate.*

**Cringley Hill:** * Possibly ON kringla. A curving hill.

**Downholme:** Dune 1086. OE dun (+ ON holmr). (The water-meadows) by the hills. 'Holme' seems to be a late addition. An 1184 version 'Dunum' means 'by the hills' or OE 'aet thaem dunum': 'holme' is thus misleading.

**Ellerton:** Alreton 1086. ON elri/OE alor + ON/OE tun. The farmstead near the alder tree.

*A small Cistercian nunnery was founded here on the banks of the Swale in the 13th century. Its ruins may be seen from the road.*

**Eskeleth:** * Possibly OE aesc/ON eski + ON hofuth. The hillside covered with ash trees.

**Faggergill:** Fagardegill 1280. ON far-garthr + ON gil. 'The sheep fold in a ravine' is a possible derivation here but the etymology is uncertain.

*There were extensive lead mines on Faggergill Moor which are said to have had 25 miles of underground railway.*

**Feetham:** Fytun 1242. ON fitjun = dative plural of ON fit. In the meadows.

*A short distance north of Feetham on the road to Arkengarthdale is the watersplash made famous by its regular appearance in the BBC TV series based on the James Herriot books 'All Creatures Great and Small'.*

**The Fleak:** * There are no early forms of this name to suggest a reliable meaning but it may be a version of the dialect word 'fleke' meaning a hurdle or fence. The Fleak is a 1650 feet high summit on the mountain highway from Askrigg in Wensleydale over to Swaledale; there might at one time have been a gate or boundary fence at this point but there is no actual evidence of this.

**Fremington:** Fremyngton 1086. OE personal name, Frema + OE ing-tun. Frema's farmstead.

*Fremington Edge, just north of the hamlet, is an impressive two-mile long limestone scar, an appropriate boundary for the National Park at this point. To the south across the valley floor are the remains of prehistoric ramparts.*

**Greets:** * ON grjot/OE greot. Stony, gravelly land.

**Grinton:** Grinton 1086. OE grene + OE tun. The green farm (i.e. with rich pasture).

*Grinton is at the dividing line between the gentle, green and wooded landscape of Lower Swaledale and the wilder moorland scenery of the Upper Valley. It has a long history: Celtic defensive ramparts and hill-forts are close by; its name indicates an Anglo-Saxon settlement; its Church, once the Mother Church for the whole of Swaledale, was a Norman foundation although its present structure is mainly 15th century; it was the centre of a flourishing coal and lead mining industry from the 16th to the 19th century with extensive relics still to be seen on the moors nearby; and it has retained a wealth of interesting old houses including the 17th century Blackburn Hall, reminders of Grinton's prosperous times as an important market town for the area.*

**Gunnerside:** Gunnersete 1304. ON personal name, Gunnar + ON sætr. Gunnar's seter.

*Gunnerside nestles beneath the sheltering hills with some of Swaledale's famous hay meadows, (each with its stone field barn), between the village and the river, an idyllic pastoral scene once the centre of an intense lead-mining industry in Gunnerside Gill. The hushes, the ruins, the debris, the mouths of the adits may still be seen but, most notable, is a well-preserved 'bousestead' where the ore was broken up and separated from the rock before being sent to the smelt mills at Blakethwaite and Old Gang, impressive even today in their sombre ruins.*

**Harkerside:** Harker 1771. Harker is a surname derived from ME herkien (meaning to eavesdrop) + ON sætr. Harker's seter.

**Hartlakes:** * ON hjortr + ON leikr. The place where harts play. (This is a reference to the arenas where the red deer indulge in their trials of strength in the rutting season).

**Haverdale:** * ON hafri + ON dalr. The valley where oats are grown.

**Healaugh:** Helagh 1260. OE heah + OE leah. The clearing in the high forest.

*Healaugh was a 12th century settlement, a forest village created by the lords of Richmond to oversee the special needs of Arkengarthdale Forest, one of the many hunting forests established by the Normans throughout the country.*

**Helwith:** Helwathe 1280. ON hella + ON vath. The ford made of flat stones.

**Hoove:** * Etymology obscure. A possible derivation is OE hufe, a hill shaped like a hood.

**Hudswell:** Hudredswelle 1086. OE personal name, Hudel + OE wella. Hudel's well.

**Ingsque:** * Etymology obscure. A possible explanation is that the first element is an ON personal name (Ingvar, Ingun etc.) + ON skogr. Ingvar's wood.

**Ivelet:** Iflythe 1301. OE personal name, Ifa + ON hlith. Ifa's hillside.

*Ivelet has a handsome 17th century stone bridge over the Swale.*

**Keld:** * ON kelda. The spring. (Until the late Middle Ages this place-name is recorded with the meaning 'The spring by the apple tree' as in the 1301 example Appeltrekelde).

*Keld is the last hamlet in Upper Swaledale. Beyond this are the bleak moorlands of Birkdale and West Stonesdale. But in Keld itself are all the features of a Dales valley: the solid sandstone buildings, the hay meadows, the field barns, and the river, here cascading over a series of falls - Kisdon Force, East Gill Force, Catrake Force and Wainwath Force - all fed by many gills tumbling down wooded ravines. In Keld, too, begins the ancient Corpse Road along which the dead were carried for burial in the only Church in Swaledale at Grinton, a road which is now a fine bridleway passing over Kisdon Hill and on to Muker and beyond.*

**Kisdon:** The second element here is almost certainly OE dun, a hill, but the first element has no satisfactory explanation.

*An 18th century version of this name - Kisdon Island - refers to the fact that the hill is surrounded by water. On the western side, following a former course of the River Swale, is a beck known as Skeb Sceugh, and on the eastern side is the River Swale in its changed course.*

*Kisdon Hill is traversed by the ancient Corpse Road (see Keld) and by the modern Pennine Way en route northwards from Thwaite to Keld.*

**Kitley Hill:** Kydalehowe 1285. ON kyr + ON dalr + ON haugr. The hill above the valley where cows are kept.

**Langthwaite:** Langethwait 1167. OE lang + ON thveit. The long clearing.

*Langthwaite is the main settlement in Arkengarthdale and has many relics of the days when it was the centre of the lead-mining industry. It has the only example in the Dales of a 'Commissioners Church', that is a Church built with funds provided by Parliament in the years following the Napoleonic Wars. Such churches are often known as Waterloo Churches.*

**Lops Wath:** * This may be a personal name or nickname derived from ON hlaup, a leap and, indirectly, a fugitive. Lop's ford.

**Low Row:** * The low row of cottages. ON lagr + OE raw.

**Maiden Castle:** *This name is given to a large number of ancient hill-forts in various parts of the country. The origin of the name is obscure. Games or rituals in which maidens took part have been suggested.

*Maiden Castle is two miles to the west of Grinton, a fortified site probably associated with the Celtic earthworks thrown across the valley floor below. There is an impressive rampart and ditch, and an avenue of stones nearby.*

**Marrick:** Marige 1086. ON marr + ON hyrggr. The ridge where horses graze.

*A Benedictine Nunnery was founded in 1156 near to a ford across the Swale to the west of Marrick. It was connected to the village by a mile-long causeway known as The Nuns' Steps. Only scant ruins of the Church now remain but parts of the Priory buildings have been converted into an Outdoor Activities Centre.*

**Marske:** Mersche 1086. OE mersc. The Marsh.

*Pillimire Bridge over Marske Beck may be a packhorse bridge but its purpose is unclear.*

**Melbecks Moor:** * The moor between the streams. ON methal (ME i melle) + ON bekkr + OE mor. Melbecks lies between Gunnerside Beck and Barney Beck.

**Muker:** Meuhaker 1274. ON mjor + ON akr. The small arable field.

*Muker is the Mecca for tourists visiting Swaledale. The village has a delightful setting on the Swale and is well furnished with shops, cafes, accommodation, a Post Office and a well-known inn. The annual Summer Fair is a traditional village Fete with Muker's own Brass Band. St. Mary's Church here is an Elizabethan foundation dating from 1580 but it received much attention from Victorian restorers. The hay meadows near Muker are the finest in the Dales: the five-mile walk to Gunnerside and back in late June is a memorable experience, not least for the 90 stiles one has to negotiate on the way. Swaledale's famous field barns are uniquely visible hereabouts; the O.S. Map shows 100 of them within a half-mile radius of Muker. A plaque on the old Grammar School commemorates its two most famous pupils, the Kearton brothers, pioneer wildlife photographers.*

**Nine Standards:** These boundary marks are just beyond the northern border of the Dales National Park and form a distinctive feature of the landscape at well over 2,000 feet. They are tall pillars of stones and the name 'standards' is derived from 'stander', a mining term for a pillar of coal left to support a roof. (ye Nine standers 1687).

**Oxnop:** Oxenhope 1301. OE oxa + OE hop. The valley where the oxen are kept.

*Low Oxnop has the finest 17th century house (1685) in Swaledale. Oxnop Scar at the summit of the road between Muker and Askrigg is a famous viewpoint.*

**Oxque:** * Etymology obscure. Possibly OE oxa + ON skogr. The wood where oxen graze.

**Pry Hill:** * Look-out hill. OE praw (ME prien, to spy) + OE hyll.

**Punchard:** * No satisfactory explanation of this name is available.

**Rampsholme:** * The watermeadow where wild garlic grows. ON holmr + ON hramsa.

**Ravenseat:** * Hrafn's hilltop. ON personal name + ON saeti.

*The hamlet of Ravenseat is Swaledale's most remote settlement, a lonely outpost in Whitsundale on the old packhorse route to Tan Hill and Teesdale. The packhorse bridge has a high humpback and retains the original cobbled surface.*

**Reeth:** Rie 1086, Ryth 1224. OE rith, aet thaem rithe. The place by the stream.

*Elegance and prosperity came to Reeth in the 18th century when the lead-mining and knitting industries began to flourish and when the construction of the turnpike brought coaching inns and townhouses whose Georgian grandeur still gives the town a special distinction. Agricultural prosperity also enabled Reeth to take full advantage of its 1695 Charter and at one time it had seven annual fairs in addition to the regular Friday market. Today with only one third of its former population it is a thriving tourist centre, the home of the Swaledale Folk Museum, a remarkable insight into many aspects of the history of the valley.*

**Richmond:** This name was bestowed on an earlier settlement by Count Alan, the Norman Earl of Richmond who built the castle here in the late 11th century. 'Richemont' was a familiar name from France and by 1108 it appears in the Richmond records as 'Richemunde' replacing the mysterious 'Hindrelac' referred to in Domesday Book in 1086.

*Richmond is dominated by its Norman castle which has stood high above the River Swale for 900 years and even today its massive ruins convey an impression of strength and power. Scolland's Hall is said to be the oldest castle hall in England and the great 12th century Keep has battlements 100 feet high which offer a splendid prospect of the town below. Elegant Georgian houses and Inns line many of the fine streets: Newbiggin, 'new' in the 12th century, New Road, 'new' in the 18th century, Finkle Street, Frenchgate and King Street, while ancient medieval wynds radiate from the Market Place. Richmond's Georgian Theatre dating from 1788 and restored in 1963 is one of the oldest active Theatres in the country. Among the many attractions in the Richmondshire Folk Museum is the vet's surgery featured in the James Herriot TV series. Richmond is just outside the National Park but it is one of the glories of Swaledale and one of England's most exciting towns.*

Richmond

19

**Riddings:** Riddinge 1287. OE rydding. The cleared land.

**Satron:** Saterom 1301. ON sætr + ON rum. Land cleared for a seter.

**Shot Lathe:** * The second element is ON hlatha, a barn. Shot is a dialect term for a ewe in poor condition but OE sceot, a steep slope, is also a possibility. A barn where such ewes were kept or a barn on a steep slope.

**Shunner Fell:** * Sjonr's mountain or a look-out hill. This could be either the genitive form Sjonar of a personal name Sjonr or ON sjon + ON fjall.

*Great Shunner Fell is adorned with no fewer than ten beacons and their presence seems to suggest that it was, indeed, a 'look-out' hill. The view from its 2,340 feet summit is splendid in all directions: to Swaledale, to Ingleborough and Penyghent and to the mountain ranges of the Lake District, with wide sweeps of undulating moorland to every horizon.*

**Skeb Sceugh:** * Possibly ON skeppa + ON skogr. The wood where beehives are kept.

**Smarber:** Smerbergh 1298. ON smjor + ON berg. The hill with rich (butter producing) pasture.

**Sour Nook:** * ON saurr + ME nok. A nook of land with sour or muddy soil.

**Stang:** * ON stong. A marker stake. This is the name of the pass on the road from Arkengarthdale to Teesdale: it was customary to mark such routes by a stake or line of stakes.

**Stolerston:** * The second element is OE tun, a farmstead, but the derivation of the first part is unexplained.

**Stonesdale:** Sconesdale 1298. The first element is probably an unrecorded personal name + ON dalr.

**Storthwaite:** Stirkthwayt 1281. OE stirc + ON thveit. The clearing where stirks (young cows or oxen) were kept.

**Stubbing:** * OE stubbing. A place cleared of tree-stumps.

**Tan Hill:** * OE tan or Icelandic teinn + OE hyll. The hill with a boundary marker.

*Tan Hill's only claim to distinction today is as the site of the highest inn in England. At 1,732 feet (536m) it is a lonely and desolate situation, with empty and almost featureless moorlands for many miles around it. As a refuge for tired walkers on the Pennine Way the Inn still has a purpose in life but Tan Hill's busy days as the meeting point of four Drove Roads and Packhorse Routes and as the centre of a coal-mining industry are long gone. The boundary stone from which it may take its name is still there and County, Parish and National Park frontiers still pass through it.*

**Thiernswood:** * This is probably 'the thorny wood' but it could also be derived from a personal name or surname: 'Thirn's wood'. OE thyrne + OE wudu.

**Thwaite:** * ON thveit. This place-name is recorded in 1301 as 'Arkeltwayt' - Arkil's clearing - and thus conforms to the more usual pattern in which 'thwaite' names are combined with either a personal name or a descriptive adjective.

*Thwaite was the birthplace of Cherry and Richard Kearton, the pioneer wildlife photographers. A decorated lintel over the cottage door commemorates this event.*

**Turf Moor Hush:** * The hush on the moor where turf (for fuel) was dug. OE turf + OE mor + dial hush.

*A hush is a ravine gouged out of the fellside by miners exploiting the mineral veins in the surface rocks. Water was dammed high on the moors and then released to scour away the vegetation, soil and loose rocks in order to reveal the mineral deposits beneath. This operation repeated many times created man-made ravines. Several 'hush' names may be found close to Turf Moor Hush and others appear near the old mines in Gunnerside Gill.*

**Wham:** * OE whamm, a marshy hollow or marshy nook. A common name in the Dales.

**Whaw:** Kiwawe 1280. ON kvi + ON hagi. An enclosure with a sheep-fold.

**Whitaside:** * ON hvitr/OE hvit + OE side. The dry or white hillside.

**Whitsundale:** * The final element is obviously ON dalr but no explanation of the first part of this name can be offered. No early version is available.

**Winterings:** * This would seem to mean 'the meadows used for winter grazing'. OE winter + ON eng.

# WENSLEYDALE
# WITH BISHOPDALE AND COVERDALE

## Wensleydale:

Wandesleydale 1142.
OE personal name,
Waendel + OE leah +
ON dalr. The valley
with Waendel's wood-
land clearing.

Middleham Castle

*Wensleydale is the only main valley in the Yorkshire Dales to be named after one of its villages rather than its river. This was not always so, however. In former times Wensleydale was often referred to as Yoredale (the valley of the River Ure) and geologists still use this term to identify a series of rocks which are comprised of limestone and sandstone, a prominent feature of the local landscape. There are many other features too which distinguish Wensleydale from the other Dales. Wensleydale is a wide fertile valley of rich pastures and prosperous farms, more suited to dairy farming than the narrow, upland dales, and for over 700 years Wensleydale butter and especially Wensleydale cheese have made this valley's name well-known far beyond the banks of the Ure. This economy enabled four market towns to flourish here for many centuries, well-protected and supported by two strong castles and two powerful abbeys. Prehistoric tribes, too, found*

22

*Wensleydale a congenial place to live as is evident from their encampments at Addleborough, Castle Dykes and in the shallows of Semer Water; the Romans built a major fort here at Bainbridge, strategically sited on the roads to Lancaster and Ilkley; the coaching days made the valley a main route across the Pennines and gave it a fine turnpike to add to the existing road. Nature had already endowed Wensleydale with two of the finest waterfalls in the country at Aysgarth and Hardraw Force, and the only natural expanse of open water in the National Park at Semer Water as well as much impressive limestone and moorland scenery. Man has, over the years, added cultivated farmlands, hedgerows and woodlands, stone walls and stone barns, and a variety of village settlements rich in domestic architecture and rural tradition.*

**Bishopdale:**   Biscoppedale 1202. OE personal name, Biscop + ON dalr. Biscop's valley.

*Bishopdale was once a glacial lake with the result that it has very fertile soil and consequently when the valley ceased to be a hunting preserve for Middleham Castle it soon acquired a population of prosperous yeoman farmers who have left a legacy of some of the finest 17th century houses in the Dales. Smelter House and New House at the head of the valley are especially notable, and others may be seen in the three villages at the valley foot - Newbiggin, Thoralby and West Burton.*

**Coverdale:**   Coverdale 1202. A Celtic river-name + ON dalr. The valley of the River Cover. (See River Cover on page 27).

*Coverdale's chief claim to fame is that it was the birthplace of Miles Coverdale whose English translation of the Bible was the basis of the Great Bible of 1538, the first complete Bible in English. All parish Churches were ordered to purchase a copy in 1540. The road through Coverdale was the main coach route from London to Richmond from the 17th century onwards and appears on the reliable Ogilvy Map of 1675.*

**Abbotside:**   * OFr abbat + OE side. The Abbot's hillside.

*Ten thousand acres here were the property of Jervaulx Abbey founded in 1145.*

**Addleborough:**   Otholburg 1153. ON personal name, Authulf + OE burh. Authulf's fort.

*Addleborough is a plateau 476m in height (1561ft) with traces of an Iron Age encampment. Below the western scar is the Devil's Stone, the relic of a legendary fight between the giant who lived on Addleborough and the Devil. The Carlow Stone and the Mermaid Stones by Semer Water were also missiles in this conflict.*

**Agglethorpe:** Aculestorp 1086. OE personal name, Aculf + ON thorp. Aculf's hamlet.

**Apedale:** Apedale 1175. On personal name, Api + dalr. Api's valley.

**Appersett:** Appeltresate 1280. OE aeppeltreow + ON sætr. The seter by the apple tree.

**Arkleside:** Arkelsit 1240. ON personal name, Arkil + ON sætr. Arkil's seter.

**Askrigg:** Ascric 1086. ON askr + ON hyrggr. Ash-tree ridge.

*Askrigg was the most important village in Wensleydale and its prosperity received a further boost with the construction of the Richmond-Lancaster Turnpike in the 1750s. Its heyday is marked by many fine 18th and 19th century houses and inns; its earlier importance is shown in its 15th century church and Market Cross; and it acquired more recent fame when Cringley House featured as Skeldale House in the James Herriot TV series. The waterfalls at Mill Gill and Whitfield Gill are nearby. A medieval bridge spans Grange Beck one mile to the east and is almost certainly connected with a grange belonging to Jervaulx Abbey.*

**Aysgarth:** Echescard 1086. ON eik + ON garthr. The enclosure among the oak trees.

*Today Aysgarth is best known for its falls, a mile-long cascade where the River Ure leaps over a succession of limestone terraces. In former days its importance stemmed from its position as the religious centre of a Wensleydale parish which covered 80,000 acres: it is probable that a Christian Church has been here since the 10th century. The Church now contains much of interest, not least two fine 15th century Screens and a Reading Desk from Jervaulx Abbey. The Yore Mill, an 18th century textile mill, aroused the hostility of early environmentalists who objected to the noise, the visual intrusion and the depletion of the waters which fed the falls: a four-storey corn and worsted mill, it now enjoys a new life as a five-storey Coach and Carriage Museum.*

**River Bain:** Bayne 1153/Bein 1218. ON beinn. The short river.

*The Bain is England's shortest river. Its two mile course from Semer Water ends near Bainbridge where it joins the Ure after cascading over a series of terraces.*

**Bainbridge:** Bainebrigg 1219. ON beinn + OE brycg/ON bryggr. The bridge over the River Bain

*The old stone houses of Bainbridge are grouped round a pleasant green*

*beautifully maintained by locally elected Trustees who succeeded the City of London as lords of the manor in the 17th century. The medieval custom of blowing a horn at dusk to guide late travellers on the moors and in the forest of Wensleydale was retained until modern times and is still occasionally revived. Bainbridge has no church but it does have a Friends Meeting House, an interestingly restored corn mill, and on nearby Brough Hill, the Roman fort of Virosidium, a key point on the road to Lancaster and Ilkley and maintained for over 300 years.*

**Bardale:**   Beredale 1280. ON bjorr + ON dalr. Beaver valley. (See note on Barbon in Dentdale, page 38).

**Bearsett:**   * The second element here is most probably ON sætr but it is impossible to suggest an equally likely origin of the first element which might be a personal name or ON berg or OE bear or none of these.

**Birkrigg:**   * ON birki + ON hryggr. Birch-tree ridge.

*Birch-trees were in abundant supply and were used for a great variety of purposes. It is, therefore, not surprising that so many place-names should include the ON birki. The fine-grained wood was easily turned and was used extensively for household utensils and furniture; it was also useful for gates, fences and farm implements. The smaller branches and twigs were in demand for baskets, hurdles, hoops and besoms, and the bark was carefully stored for the tanning industry. The Spring sap was drawn off to make a very potent spirit!*

**Blean:**   Blaynbeck 1153. ON blaeingr (+ ON bekkr). The dark stream.

**Borwins:**   * OE burgaesn. A cairn, usually associated with a burial place.

**Braidley:**   OE brad + OE leah. The broad forest clearing.

**Braithwaite:**   Brathoit 1190/Braytwayt 1301. ON breithr + thveit. Broad clearing.

*Braithwaite Hall, a National Trust property, is a 17th century hall now a working farmhouse. It contains oak panelling and staircase, fine fireplaces and a stone-flagged hall. It may be seen by arrangement with the tenant.*

**Brough Hill:**   Burg 1218. OE burh. The fort.

*This was the site of the Roman fort of Virosidium, a garrison for 500 men and manned for most of the time from AD80 to AD395. It was an important strategic base from which to control the rebellious Brigantes and to protect the road to Lancaster and Ilkley, and possibly to oversee the lead-mines in Arkengarthdale.*

**Burtersett:**   Beurtresate 1280. ME bur-tre + ON sætr. The seter by the elder-tree. Bortree is the northern word for the elder-tree.

*The elder was a highly revered tree as every part had some medicinal value. For 2,000 years it was regarded as everyone's medicine chest - and every boy's popgun! Between 1860 and 1930 the Burtersett quarries produced over 15,000 tons of high quality flagstones each year and they may now be seen in local farms, barns and houses, in flagged footpaths and in many of the milltowns of Lancashire .*

**West Burton:** Burton 1086. OE burh-tun. The fortified farmstead. 'West' was added later to distinguish this place from the other Burton (Constable Burton) nine miles away to the east.

*West Burton has a poor historical heritage: it has no ancient church, it never acquired a market charter, it has no distinguished architecture and it lies on no route of trade or communication. But it does have charm in its cottages grouped round its green, in its natural setting, in its waterfall and in its packhorse bridge over the Walden Beck.*

**Caldbergh:** Caldber 1086. ON kaldr + ON berg. The cold hill.

**Carlton-in-Coverdale:** Carleton 1086. ON karl + ON tun. The freeman's farmstead. (See Coverdale, page 23).

*There are several groups of 'freemen' in Norse society, the most numerous and most important being the 'bondi' or independent freeman farmers who were the most influential men in the local 'thing' or assembly which made the laws. Carlton is the main settlement in Coverdale and, as its array of 17th century houses indicates, it had a tradition of prosperous yeomen.*

**Carperby:** Chirprebi 1086. OIr personal name, Cairpre + ON by. Cairpre's farm.

*Carperby is one of Wensleydale's linear villages with a single main street which widens to accommodate the green with a 17th century Market Cross. An impressive Friends' Meeting House recalls the days when Carperby was one of the valley's important centres of Quakerism. The Wheatsheaf Inn has acquired recent fame as the inn where James Herriot spent his honeymoon in the TV series 'All Creatures Great and Small'. The name of this inn is a reminder that corn was grown in Wensleydale not so long ago. One mile to the north-west a remarkably well preserved group of ancient strip lynchets - terraces levelled in gradations for ploughing - indicate that corn was also grown very much earlier too.*

**Castle Bolton:** Bodeltun 1086. OE bothl-tun. An enclosure with buildings, i.e. a village. The castle was built in 1379 and added to the name.

*The 14th century castle of Richard Scrope dominates the valley even today when it is only a shadow of its former glory. Mary, Queen of Scots, was imprisoned here in 1568-69 and her bed-chamber may be seen. The castle also has an impressive great hall and a restored horse mill. It is open from March to November.*

**Castle Dykes:** * OE castel + OE dic. The fort with the ramparts or embankments.

*Castle Dykes is a Bronze Age 'henge' or circular earthwork some 200 feet (61m) in diameter which may have been a viewing platform for ceremonies taking place on the central mound which is separated from the embankment by an inner ditch. It is one of the most important ancient sites in the Yorkshire Dales.*

**Cocklake Side:** le Cokelayke 1305. OE cocc + ON leikr/ME cock-lake + OE side. The hillside where the grouse or woodcock gather for display.

**Cogill:** Cottkeld 13th c. OE cot + ON kelda. The cottage by the spring.

**Coleby:** * This is probably Koli's farm. ON personal name + ON by.

**Cotescue:** Scotescogh 1510. OE Scott + ON skogr. Scott's wood or the Scotsman's wood. This may refer to a personal name or to a nationality.

**Cotterdale:** Cottesdale 1266/Coterdale 1301. OE cot/ON kot + ON dalr. The valley with the huts or cottages.

*Cotterdale Beck has several waterfalls the most notable of which is Cotter Force easily approached by a short walk along the beck from the road a mile west of Hawes.*

**Countersett:** Constansate 1280. OFr personal name, Constance + ON sætr Constance's seter.

*Countersett Hall (1650) with its fine two-storey porch and beautiful mullioned windows is just one of the well-preserved 17th century houses here. The village has a strong Quaker tradition and the Friend's Meeting House has associations with the influential Robinson family, prominent among Quakers in the 17th century.*

**River Cover:** Couer 1279. This is a Celtic river-name meaning 'the river in the hollow'.

**Coverdale:** See page 23.

**Coverham:** Covreham 1086. Cover + OE ham. The homestead by the River Cover.

*Coverham Abbey was founded in 1202 as a house for the Premonstratensian (or white) canons. Three piers and two arches remain from the 14th century buildings, and the early 16th century Gatehouse has been incorporated into a 17th century residence which itself has several nine-light windows. The property is in private grounds but may be seen from a public bridleway nearby. Coverham also produced the now rarely found Coverdale cheese made from Coverdale milk.*

**Cubeck:** * This name might be derived from OE cu and ON bekkr. The stream where the cows gather.

**Dodd Fell:** * ME dodde + ON fjall. The hill with a round summit, often the shoulder of a larger hill.

**Drumaldrace:** * The etymology here is obscure. The first element could be the Celtic word' drum', a wooded ridge, as in several Scottish place-names. The second element may be derived from a personal name (as in Drumalban, 'Alban's ridge') but it is not possible to be more precise.

**Flamstone Pin:** * This may be derived from the OIr personal name Flann + stan. Flann's stone: cf Falnshaw also in Yorkshire. OE pinn = a pointed object or a pinnacle.

**Fleensop:** Flemmishope 1240. The first element is probably an unknown personal name; the second is OE hop, a small overhanging valley.

**Floshes Hill:** * ME flosshe = a swamp. Probably 'the swampy hill'.

**Fossdale:** Fossedale 1280. ON fors + ON dalr. The valley with a waterfall (Hardraw Force).

**Gammersgill:** Gamelscale 1388. ON personal name Gamel + ON skali. Gamel's shieling.

**Gayle:** Seldagile 1280. OE slaed + ON dalr + ON gil. The ravine in Sleddale. Gayle is probably derived from ON geil, the narrow valley (of Gayle Beck.)

*Gayle is a village of cottages and narrow alleyways, once a busy centre of the cottage textile industry. The houses in Beckstones were carding and combing houses and Gayle Mill was successively a knitting mill, a cotton mill, a wollen mill and a saw mill. A quarry nearby produced flagstones not only for many towns and houses but also for several local footpaths, one of which goes across the fields to the church at Hawes.*

**Hardraw:** Hardrawe 1606. OE herde + OE raw. The shepherds' row of cottages.

*The waterfall at Hardraw, Hardraw Force, is approached through the Green Dragon Inn and along a good pleasant path to a natural amphitheatre where the water of Fossdale Gill plunges 96ft (27m) in the highest clear fall in England above ground. The wooded amphitheatre is the scene of brass band concerts in the summer months making full use of the excellent acoustics here.*

**Harland:** Harlande 1282. OE har + OE land. The land with many tumuli or heaps of stones.

**Harmby:** Hernebi 1086. ON personal name, Hjarne + ON by. Hjarn's farm.

**Hawes:** Le Thouse 1307/Hawes 1614. ON hals. The pass through the hills.

> *Hawes is at the head of Wensleydale, 850 feet above sea level, the junction of roads leading to Swaledale, Garsdale, Langstrothdale, Dentdale and Ingleton: it could not have been more aptly named. It emerged as a remote hamlet in the Forest of Wensleydale in the 14th century but did not develop until the growth of packhorse trade along all these routes qualified it to receive a market charter in 1700. The arrival of the Richmond-Lancaster coach road in 1795 and of the valley railway in the 1870s made Hawes the commercial capital of Upper Wensleydale well provided with inns, hotels, shops, manufacturers, services of all kinds and an important auction mart. It became famous for its Wensleydale cheese factory and for its rope works. The former Railway Station now houses The Dales Countryside Museum which includes the unrivalled collection assembled by Marie Hartley and Joan Ingilby.*

**Hell Gill:** See in the Dentdale/Garsdale section (page 41).

**Helm:** * OE helm. The summit of a hill.

**Hestholme:** * ON hestr + ON holmr. The water-meadow where horses were pastured. Of Oxenholme, Gooseholme, Kidholme etc.

**Hindlethwaite:** Hyndelaythwayt 1388. OE hind + OE leah + ON thveit. The forest clearing where hinds graze.

**Horrabank:** * OE horu + OE banke. The dirty or muddy hillslope.

**Horse House:** * This improbable name is generally believed to owe its origin to the fact that this was a resting place for packhorses en route from Middleham to Wharfedale. It is tempting with this name to make a comparison with Haws House on the route between Bainbridge and Ingleton - i.e. The house on the pass, but topographically this is less convincing in Coverdale as the 'pass' at 835ft is followed by a descent of only 40ft before the road rises again for several miles to reach over 1,650ft before the final descent into Wharfedale. OE/ON hals, a pass through the hills, is just possible but in the absence of any early versions of the name it remains uncertain.

**Jervaulx:** Jorvalle 1135. Fr. 'Jor' = Yore or Ure + Fr. val (pl. vaux). (The place in) the valley of the River Ure.

> *Jervaulx Abbey was founded as a Cistercian house in 1145 and in the following centuries acquired lands which gave it effective ownership of most of Wensleydale. It also established a horse-breeding farm at Horton-in-Ribblesdale. At the time of the Dissolution the abbot of Jervaulx, like the abbot of Fountains, paid with his life for resisting the Crown's officers*

*and for conspiring to foment rebellion. The property is now privately owned but the public are able to see the impressive ruins of the chapter-house and dormitories.*

**Kidstones:**  Kydestanes 1270. ME klde + OE stan. The rocks where young goats gather.

*Kidstones itself is near the head of Bishopdale but the name is also given to Kidstones Causeway, part of the Roman road from Bainbridge into Wharfedale.*

**Lenacre:**  Langacre 1547. OE lang + OE aecer. The long plot of cultivated land.

**Leyburn:**  Leborne 1086. OE leah + OE burna. The stream in the woodland clearing.

*Leyburn's pre-eminence as the commercial centre for much of Wensleydale dates only from the 19th century with the arrival first of the main turnpike road and then of the railway. It is primarily a late Georgian and early Victorian town but little remains of what must once have been an imposing group of houses and shops round the spacious market place. From 'Leyburn Shawl', a grassy limestone terrace, may be seen a quite splendid panorama of Wensleydale. The term 'shawl' was given to the process of winnowing corn and to the scoop used for this purpose.*

**Litherskew:**  Litherskewe 1606. ON hlith + ON skogr. The wood on the hillslope.

**Locker Tarn:**  * The etymology here is obscure. The name may be derived from the OE locere = a shepherd and ON tjorn. The shepherd's tarn. Other possibilities are OE lacu = a stream and ON leikr = to play.

**Marsett:**  Mouresate 1283. ON personal name, Maurr + ON sætr. Maurr's seter. ON maurr also means 'ant' and the name Maurr may be derived from this.

*Marsett is the best starting point for an exploration of the remote and largely unfrequented side valley of Bardale along a footpath by Bardale Beck.*

**Melmerby:**  Melmerbi 1086. ON personal name Melmor + ON by. Melmor's farm.

**Middleham:**  Medelei 1086/Midelham 1184. OE middel + OE ham. The middle homestead. (The topographical references of 'middle' are not at all obvious).

*The keep of Middleham castle (1170) is one of the largest in England, an appropriate stronghold for the Nevilles and especially for King Richard 111 whose power-base this was from 1472 - 1485. The impressive ruins of the castle today still fully convey the former strength and importance of*

*Middleham. Nearby is the 13th century chapel of St. Alkelda which was made a Collegiate Foundation in 1478: Charles Kingsley was its last canon in the mid-19th century. Middleham acquired its market charter in 1389 and in Georgian times became one of the most prosperous and urbane towns in the north, a hey-day reflected in the elegant Georgian houses in the market place and in the fine coaching inns nearby. Middleham today is perhaps best known as the centre of an important race-horse establishment.*

**Mossdale:**  * ON mosi + ON dalr. The boggy valley.

**Nappa:**  Napars 1086/Nappay 1251. OE hnaepp = OE (ge) haeg. The bowl-shaped enclosure.

*Nappa Hall is one of the rare examples in the Dales of a fortified house built in the 15th century as a protection against Scottish raiders: cf Bardon Tower. Nappa Hall is not open to the public but may be viewed from a public footpath close by.*

**Naughtberry Hill:**  * ON knutr + OE berie. Cloudberry Hill. (The northern name for the cloudberry is the knoutberry or knotberry).

**Newbiggin:**  Newbigging 1230. OE niwe + ME bigging. The new building or outhouse.

**Penhill:**  Penle 1202. OWelsh penn/Br penno + OE hyll. The hill. (The OE 'hyll' was added superfluously by the Saxon settlers to whom the British word 'penno' was incomprehensible).

*Penhill was a former beacon site in the chain of beacons across the Pennines.*

**Preston-under-Scar:**  Prestun 1086. OE preost + OE tun + ON sker. The priest's farmstead under the scar: i.e. Preston Scar.

**Raydale;**  Radale 1307. ON ra + ON dalr. Roebuck valley.

**Redmire:**  Ridemare 1086. OE hreod + OE mere. The pool covered with reeds.

*Redmire's church has a fine Norman doorway but the village is essentially an industrial village which developed with the lead mines, coal mines and quarries in the 18th and 19th centuries. Extensive scars from these workings may be seen on the moors to the north covering an area of more than three square miles. A mile to the south and just within the National Park is the small waterfall on the River Ure known as Redmire Force.*

**Routen Gill/Beck:**  * The roaring ravine/beck. OE hrutan + ON gil/bekkr.

**Scrafton:**  Skrafton 1086. OE scraef + OE tun. The farmstead in a hollow.

**Seata:**  Seata Hill 1847. ON sætr + ON haugr. The seter on a hill.

**Sedbusk:**  Setebuskste 1280. ON sætr + ON buskr. The seter by the bush.

**Semer Water:** Semerwater 1153. OE sae + OE mere + OE waeter. The lake. (All three elements in this name have the same meaning).

*Semer Water is the largest natural lake in the Dales National Park, half a mile long and two miles in circumference. It is a glacial lake held back by a moraine. The level of the lake was lowered in 1937 to reveal evidence of a prehistoric village along an earlier shoreline, so giving new life to the old legend that a wanderer here seeking food and a night's shelter was refused at every house but one so he pronounced a curse on the place which resulted in such a downpour of rain that the lake rose and drowned the entire village except the one house which had taken him in. The lake is now a popular place for swimmers, anglers, windsurfers and over-wintering wildfowl.*

**Simonstone:** Simoundstane 1301. OE personal name, Sigemund + OE stan. Sigemund's Stone.

**Skell Gill:** * ON skali or ON skjallr + ON gil. The ravine with a shieling or the ravine with a resounding stream.

**Slapestones Wath:** * ON sleipr + OE stan + ON vath. The ford with the slippery stones.

**Sleddale:** * OE slaed + ON dalr. The valley. (Both elements have the same meaning).

**Snaizeholme:** Snaysum 1280. ON sneis (pl. sneisum). The place covered in twigs.

**Sorrelsykes:** * OE sorell + OE sic. The water meadow where sorrel grows.

*The various types of sorrel were highly valued for both medicinal and culinary purposes, notably in the treatment of scurvy and kidney problems and as an eye lotion. As a green sauce to garnish pork or goose it was held in high esteem. It appears in many place-names.*

**Spennithorne:** Speningetorp 1086. The first element is most probably a personal name + ing; the second is ON thorp, an outlying farm or hamlet.

**Stake Moss:** Steks 1663. OE staca + OE mos. The boggy ground marked out with stakes. (The route of the Roman road from Ilkley to Bainbridge passes across this moss which clearly had to be marked out with direction stakes).

**Stalling Busk:** Stalunbusk 1283 .OFr estalon + ON buskr. The stallion's bush.

*The Roman road from Bainbridge to Wharfedale passes near Stalling Busk before climbing over Stakes Moss to the Kidstones Pass. Half a mile to the north of the hamlet are the ruins of a small chapel which served as the church for Stalling Busk from 1603 to 1909.*

**Stony Raise:** La Staynrayse 1307. OE stan + ON hreysi. The stone cairn.

(Ancient enclosures are in this vicinity with what has obviously been a very substantial cairn nearby).

**Swinacote:** Swynewathcot 1298. OE swin + ON vath + OE cot. The cottage by the ford where the swine cross.

**Swineside:** Swinsate 1240. OE swin + ON sætr. The seter where swine were kept.

**Swinithwaite:** Swiningithwait 1202. On svithingr + ON thveit. The clearing made by burning. The first element could be a personal name + ing.

**Thoralby:** Turoldesbi 1086. ON personal name, Thoraldr + ON by. Thorald's farm.

*There are several excellent examples of 17th century Dales houses here, notably Old Hall (1641). A factory to make Wensleydale cheese was set up here by Alfred Rowntree in the early years of the 20th century.*

**Thoresby:** Toresbi 1086. ON personal name, Thorir + ON by. Thorir's farm.

**Thornton Rust:** Torenton 1086/Thorneton Ruske 1153. OE thorn + OE tun + ON personal name, Hrosskell. (Hrosskell held this manor and appears in Domesday Book as Roschil). Roschil's farmstead among the thorn bushes.

**Ulfer's Gill:** * This is most probably an ON personal name, Ulfr + ON gil. Ulfr's ravine .

**Ulshaw:** Woluesbowe 1158. The first element could be an ON personal name, Ulfr but it is more probably ON ulfr, a wolf, replacing OE wulf as in the 1158 version. The second element is ON haugr. Ulfr's hill or wolf hill.

**River Ure:** Jor 1140/Yor 1175/Yeure 1530. A Celtic river-name, Isura, which has a general meaning of 'power', whether physical or spiritual, and so the name Ure may be interpreted as 'the strong river' or 'the Holy river'. (See Yoredale, page 35).

*The Ure has its source some 2,000 feet above sea level on the desolate flanks of Abbotside Common, flowing at first to the west and then to the south before finally turning on its main easterly course near the lonely Moorcock Inn. From this point it is the central topographical feature of Wensleydale - or Yoredale - gathering along its way the waters of many becks and rivers flowing from the moors and from the tributary valleys. After Middleham Castle and Jervaulx Abbey it pursues a less scenic course until, at the end of its 60 mile journey, it joins the Swale and the Nidd to form the Ouse as it flows into the City of York. The bridge over the Ure at Ulshaw is dated 1674 and is perhaps the most attractive in the whole of Wensleydale.*

**Wainwath:** * OE waegn + ON vath. The ford used by wagons.

**Walden:** Waldene 1270. OE walh + OE denu. The valley where the serfs or aliens (i.e. the Britons) live. Many place-names have the element 'walh' which is often interpreted as 'serfs', and refers to the pockets of British settlement which remained after the Anglo-Saxon colonisation.

*Walden is a remote, deeply cut and enclosed valley, and although it became more populous in later centuries, as the 17th century farms and buildings indicate, it must have offered a refuge in the 8th century for the fugitive Celts driven out of the better lands by the advancing Saxons.*

**Wasset Fell:** * The etymology here is obscure. A comparison with the name Whasset south of Kendal (which is quite fully documented) would suggest either a derivation from OE hwaes/ON hvass + OE heaford, meaning a pointed headland (not topographically improbable here), or from the OE personal name, Hwaessa + OE heafod. Hwaessa's headland.

**Wegber:** * The second element here is probably OE beorg/ON berg = a hill, and the first is probably an unknown descriptive adjective.

**Wensley:** Wendreslaga 1086. OE personal name, Waendel + OE leah. Waendel's forest clearing.

*Wensley's importance in medieval times may be deduced from the fact that it gave its name to the whole valley of Wensleydale thus replacing Yoredale derived from the River Ure. Wensley acquired its market charter as early as 1202 and its pre-eminence gave it a fine 14th century bridge and the most outstanding church in or near the National Park. Two grave stones from the 10th century indicate an early foundation but the present church is mainly from about 1300 and it clearly gained from the patronage of the Scropes of Bolton Castle whose family pews still remain, together with a medieval reliquary, a two-decker pulpit and much fine woodwork including a screen from Easby Abbey. Public footpaths through the parklands of Bolton Hall provide Wensley with an additional attraction*

**West Burton:** See page 26.

**Widdale:** Withdale 1217. ON vithr + ON dalr. The wooded valley.

*The 18th century road builders who constructed the Ingleton-Wensleydale section of the Lancaster-Richmond Turnpike considered the route taken by the Romans over Cam Fell to be altogether too hazardous in winter and chose the wide valley of Widdale instead. Widdale is today perhaps the most heavily forested of all the Dales.*

**Witton East and West:** Witun 1086 (East). ON vithr + OE/ON tun. The farmstead in the wood.

*East Witton's early prosperity depended largely on its proximity to Jervaulx Abbey (it acquired a market charter in 1307) and on the patronage of the Earls of Ailesbury whose family succeeded the*

*Cistercians in ownership of the Abbey estates. The cottages were rebuilt early in the 19th century but on precisely the same plan as in 1627; a new Church was also built - the ruins of the old one probably indicate the centre of the original settlement and the site of the market. Braithwaite Hall lies two miles to the west (see Braithwaite page 25). West Witton's fame now rests chiefly on its appearance in the TV series 'All Creatures Great and Small'. James Herriot and his friends met regularly in the Wensleydale Heifer to enjoy its hospitality. Of considerably older vintage is Saint Barthololew's Fair held on 24th August.*

**Woodale:** Wulvedale 1223. OE wulf + ON dalr. The valley where wolves live.

**Worton:** Werton 1086. OE wyrt-tun. The herb or vegetable garden.

**Yoredale:** This name was in former days often used for Wensleydale and is derived directly from the River Ure (see page 33). It is also used as a geological term to describe the type of limestone and sandstone rocks which occur locally.

**Yorescott:** * OE cot. The cottage by the River Ure.

# DENTDALE AND GARSDALE

Dentdale

**Dentdale:** The valley of the River Dent (now named the Dee which is linguistically a back formation of Dent). The name is recorded in 1200 as Dereta, a Celtic river-name probably derived from the Welsh 'dwfr' meaning water and when associated with streams usually implies 'holy' or 'sacred' water + ON dalr (see Dent p40).

*DENTDALE is distinguished from other Yorkshire Dales by two features: the geological fault which divides the valley, with the Pennine limestone on one side and Lakeland slate on the other; and, secondly, by the pattern of isolated farmsteads which contrasts with the clustered cottages of village settlements elsewhere. Walkers on the Dales Way and cyclists on the Dales Cycle Way pass along the entire length of this valley from the source of the Dee, near the Dent Head viaduct of the Carlisle-Settle railway, to Sedbergh where the river joins the Rawthey. On their way they pass through a quiet pastoral countryside, never very far from the river, and with every opportunity to see a variety of birds and other wildlife. The village of Dent is a fine example of an old and attractive settlement surviving unspoilt and vibrant into the modern age. Sedbergh, the largest town in the Yorkshire Dales, still retains all the character of a small country market town. Nestling under the massive bulk of the Howgill Fells, Sedbergh was the cradle of the Quaker Movement in the 17th century: a short distance to the North is Firbank Fell where George Fox preached in the open air to more than a thousand followers and, on the outskirts of the town, is Brigflatts, perhaps the most handsome Quaker Meeting House still in regular use.*

## Garsdale:
Garcedale 1240. This is derived from the ON personal name, Garthr + ON dalr. Garth's valley.

*GARSDALE is the deep narrow valley of the fast-flowing River Clough which is crossed by numerous bridges leading to the scattered farmsteads whose names so clearly reflect their Norse origins. The valley acquired a turnpike road in the 18th century but before that it could have changed little since the early settlements were made. To the west, Garsdale, at certain points, enjoys unrivalled views of the Howgills, and northwards from Garsdale Head an ancient highway leads to mysterious Mallerstang and Pendragon Castle.*

**Aisgill:** * ON eisa + ON gil. The ravine with the rushing stream.
> *Aisgill marks the summit of the Settle-Carlisle railway at 356m (1,169ft).*

**Arant Haw:** * The second element here is ON haugr, a hill. Arant is so far unexplained.

**Arten Gill:** * The first element here may be a personal name but no evidence is available; the second element is ON gil.
> *This remote spot was in the 18th century the site of a woollen mill which at a later date produced a highly polished marble from the local limestone which was much in demand for the new town houses of Victorian England. This fine marble was also used in building the Arten Gill viaduct on the Settle-Carlisle railway in the 1870's.*

**Aye Gill:** Hay Gill 1771. ON a + ON gil. The ravine with a stream.

**Backstone Gill:** Baxtongill 1592. OE baec-stan + ON gil. The ravine where bakestones are found.
> *Bakestones or bakstones were large flat stones on which the traditional north-country thin unleavened oat bread or clapbread was baked. This*

*type of bread, still widely used in Scandinavia, was brought by the Norsemen and was baked in every farm kitchen until modern times.*

**Barbon:**  Berebrunn 1086. ON bjorr + ON brunnr. The beaver stream.

*The beaver was already an 'endangered species' in Britain in the 10th century and few place-names refer to it. In 940 a beaver fur was valued at 15 times that of a fox, a sure sign of scarcity. Less than 200 years later the beaver was extinct in this country. (See Barbondale and Barben Beck).*

**Barkin:**  Barkerkin 1278. ON personal name, Borkr + ON kinn. Borkr's steep hillside.

**Baugh Fell:**  Bawghell 1592. OE balg + OE hyll. The round hill.

**Birks:**  * ON birki. The birch trees. A common place-name in the North.

**Blades:**  * Blades is a local surname. The Sedbergh Records refer to one 'John Blayds, a poor man'.

**Blands:**  * Bland is a local surname (John Bland 1608) but this name may be derived from ON blanda, a term used in Orkney and Shetland for a mixture of buttermilk and water, perhaps referring to the churned up water in a nearby stream.

**Borrett:**  Borhead 1608. OE bor + OE heafod. The point at the end of a ridge.

*Borrett was the home of Justice Gervase Benson where George Fox attended his first Quaker Meeting in the Sedbergh area in 1652.*

**Bramaskew:**  Brameskew 1597. OE brom + ON haugr + ON skogr. The wood on the broom covered hill.

**Brant Fell:**  * ON brant + ON fjall. The steep hill.

**Branthwaite:**  Bramthwat 1295. OE brom + ON thveit. The clearing among the broom.

**Brigflatts:**  * The bridge over the level fields. Probably a reference to a division in the common field marked by a hard causeway. The local dialect 'flat' refers specifically to a field division. OE brycg + ON flat/Dial flat.

*Brigflatts Meeting House is generally regarded as the most handsome Quaker Meeting House in England. It was built in 1675, is still in regular use, and has some exceptionally fine woodwork.*

**Brockholes Gill:**  Brokhole 1377. OE brocc-hol + ON gil. The ravine with the badger setts.

**The Calf:**  * 'Calf' is often used to indicate a small object adjacent to a larger one when it does not obviously refer to the animal. It is not clear why 'The Calf' which is the highest point in the Howgill Fells should have acquired this name. A possible explanation may be that once there may have been larger stones here to mark the county boundary which ran nearby.

**Carlin Gill:**  Kerlingile 1220. ON kerling + ON gil. The old crone's ravine.

**Castle Haw:**  * Derived from OE castel + ON haugr. The hill with a castle.

*This hill above Sedbergh was the site of a Norman motte and bailey castle.*

**Castley:**  Castelhou 1220. OE castel + ON haugr. The hill with a fort. (Occasionally in place-names it seems that any heap of tumbled stones was mistaken for the ruins of a fort).

**Catholes:**  * OE catt + OE hol. The hollows where the wild cats had their dens.

*The wild cat was common in this part of Britain in the late 18th century and was described by one guide-book writer as 'near the size of a fox' and 'grey with black strokes across the back'. It was a 'most fierce animal' living among rocks and in hollow trees. It was extinct here by the mid-19th century, the last one being shot on Great Mell Fell near Ullswater.*

**Cautley:**  Cawtleye 1574. ME cautell + OE leah. The woodland clearing with a fish-trap.

*Cautley Spout is a cascade of water falling approximately 700 feet (213m), one of the highest falls in the country. The Cross Keys Inn nearby is owned by the National Trust and dates from about 1600.*

**Clint:**  Clintel 1648. ODan klint. A crag or rocky cliff.

**River Clough:**  * OE cloh = ravine. The reference is to the narrow valley in which the river flows and it may refer especially to Clough Force, the waterfall about Clough itself.

*At Danny Bridge, near Garsdale Foot, the River Clough surges through a gorge which is of special geological interest and is part of the two-mile long Sedgwick Geology Trail, created to commemorate Adam Sedgwick the eminent geologist who was born in Dent in 1785.*

**Coventree:**  * This is the northern dialect word for the guelder rose. A covintree was also a tree where people gathered; a meeting place

**Cowgill:**  Callgill 1592. Apparently the dialect word 'caul' meaning a dam or weir to divert water for a mill-race + ON gil. The ravine with a weir.

**Cowper Gill:**  * OE coupare + ON gil. Cooper's ravine. Cooper may be a surname or an occupation.

**Crook of Lune:**  * ON krokr. A sharp bend in the River Lune.

*The famous narrow bridge over the Lune here is certainly of 16th century date and may be even older. It has two semi-circular arches and is surely one of the most beautiful and picturesque bridges in the country. It once marked the county boundary between Westmorland and Yorkshire.*

**Dandry Garth:**  * Andrew's enclosure. ON garthr.

**Dandry Mire:**  * Andrew's marsh. ON myrr.

**Danny Bridge:** * Andrew's bridge. OE brycg. Dandry and Danny are pet forms of Andrew or variations of the nickname 'Dander'.

**River Dee:** Dereta 1200. The modern name of the River Dent in Dentdale. The origin of the river-name is believed to be the Welsh 'dwfr' meaning 'water' and when applied to rivers implies 'holy' or 'sacred' water. 'Dee' is a back formation of 'Dent'.

**Dent:** Denet 1202. This may be an ancient river name which is now lost or it may be derived from OIr 'dind', a hill.

*Narrow cobbled streets give a unique charm to Dent and its principal building, St. Andrew's Church, a mainly 15th century structure, has a magnificent setting. In the 18th and 19th centuries the town had a thriving knitting industry with a ready market in Kendal. Its most famous son was Adam Sedgwick (1785-1873), the renowned geologist who is commemorated by the Geology Trail in Garsdale and by a granite memorial by the church near the grammar school which he attended. Dent station on the scenic Settle to Carlisle railway is the highest main-line station in Britain at 1,150 feet.*

**Dillicar:** Dylcar 1379. OE dile + OE aecer. The field where dill is grown.

*Dill was well-known in Anglo-Saxon England as a pickling herb, as a flavouring for soups and stews and as a soothing medication for babies and it appears prominently in the medieval Herbals. A guide to its cultivation is found in a 13th century Gardening Book.*

**Dowbiggin:** Dowbigging 1325. OE dufa or ON personal name, Dufa + ME bigging: 'dufa' is more usual in Yorkshire place-names but ON personal name is also possible. The dove house or Dufa's buildings.

**Dummacks:** * This is probably 'the dung-heap', from northern dialect 'dummock'.

**Ecker Secker Gill:** Hecker-seker 1540. The local surname, Hacker + OE aecer. Hacker's field + ON gil. See Hacker Gill.

**Fawcett:** * OE fag + OE side. The colourful hillside. (The same name in Westmorland is recorded as Fakside in 1256).

**Fawes:** * This might be similar to Faw in Westmorland: OE (ge)fall, a woodland clearing.

**Firbank:** Frethebanke 1225. OE fyrthe + OE banke. A wooded hillside.

*The woods have long disappeared from Firbank and it was on a bare hillside here that, standing on a great rock now known as Fox's pulpit, George Fox in 1652 preached to about 1,000 people. A commemorative tablet on the rock records the occasion. Fox stayed at nearby Draw Well Farm, a name derived from ME drawe-welle, a well from which water is drawn up by bucket.*

**Flust:** * The origin of this name is obscure. A similar name near Kendal - Flustey - is derived from the ON personal name Floki (Flokesti 1184) and this may also apply here. An old route to the highway to Kirkby Stephen passed this way: Floki's path? ON stigr.

**Frostow:** Frostwray 1535. ON personal name, Frosti + ON vra. Frosti's nook.

**Gastack:** * The dialect word 'tack' refers to land hired as cattle pasture and this may be the second element in this name. The first part is unexplained.

**Gawthrop:** Gawthorpe 1592. ON gaukr + ON thorp. Cuckoo hamlet. (Gaukr was also a personal name: this would give 'Gaukr's hamlet').

*This charming hamlet is on the narrow road leading to Barbondale, a short steep-sided valley along the Dent geological fault with Silurian slate on one side and Craven limestone on the other. Barbondale is one of the wilder valleys, remote and uninhabited, threaded by the waters of Barkin Beck which is partly fed by water from several chalybeate wells on High Barbon Fell.*

**Grisedale:** * ON gris + ON dalr. The valley where young pigs were kept.

**Hacker Gill:** * Hacker is a local surname which originally meant a woodcutter or one who makes hacks or mattocks + ON gil. Hacker's ravine.

**Harbour Gill:** Harbergill 1660. OE here-beorg/ON herbergi + ON gil. The ravine near the inn (although this might be no more than a shelter).

**Hebblethwaite:** Hebletwayt 1379. Dial 'hebble' = a simple plank bridge + ON thveit. The clearing by the plank bridge.

*Hebblethwaite Hall and its adjoining buildings are mainly of the 17th century. In the following century a woollen mill was established here, later converted into a bobbin mill. Robert Foster, the Quaker social reformer and friend of William Wordsworth, lived here.*

**Hell Gill Beck:** Helbeck 1504. ON hellir + ON bekkr (+ON gil). The ravine with a river flowing from a deep recess.

*Hell Gill Bridge crosses a deep limestone gorge in this wild and remote spot on the old county boundary. The busy drove road between Kirky Stephen and Swaledale, known as The Highway, once passed over this well-named ravine.*

**Helmside:** Helmside 1672. OE helm + OE side. The hill with a cattle shelter.

**Hewthwaite:** Hothwayt 1256. ON hor + thveit. The high clearing.

**Hining:** * ON hegning. An enclosure.

**Hobdale Beck:** * ME hobbe + ON dalr + ON bekkr. The stream in the valley haunted by hobgoblins.

**Hollins:** * OE holegn. The holly tree. A common place-name in the north.

*The holly tree was once held in particular reverence as a protection against evil spirits and as a traditional feature of both the pagan and the Christian Yuletide and Christmas festivals. The young shoots were also fed to sheep to give the mutton an attractive flavour. Thomas West wrote in his guidebook that the land was 'so covered with these trees as to have the appearance of a forest of hollies'.*

**The Howgill Fells:** Holegile 1235. OE hol + ON gil (+ ON fjall). The hills with deep ravines.

*The Howgills are 40 square miles of rounded, grassy, unenclosed hills near the borders of the Dales National Park. A characteristic feature is a series of deep ravines, most impressive in the light cast by the morning or evening sun. This is lonely country, frequented only by Rough Fell sheep, birds of prey and the occasional fell-walker. There are fine views of the Pennines, the Lakeland Fells, the limestone heights of the Dales, and the distant sea. Alfred Wainwright believed that 'There is no more extensive panorama in England than this'.*

**Ingmire:** * ON eng + ON myrr. The boggy meadow.

**Knoutberry Haw:** * ON knottr-ber + ON haugr. Cloudberry hill. (The northern dialect word for the cloudberry is the knotberry).

**Knudmaning:** * The meadow belonging to Knut's manservant. 'Man' added to a personal name was a feature of feudal society. + ON eng.

**Lamps Moss:** * The first element is unexplained; the second is ON mos. This name is recorded in 1652 as 'Lampes Mosse where Richmondshire and Westmerland are divided'. The ancient route from Swaledale to the Eden Valley crossed the county boundary at this point.

**Lea Yeat:** Leeyete 1636. OE leah + OE geat. The gate by the woodland clearing.

**Lunds:** * ON lundr. The small wood or grove (often with religious associations).

**Mallerstang:** Malvestang 1228. Wel. moel-fre + ON stong. The bare hill with a landmark pole.

*Mallerstang Forest, a bare and severe landscape, marked the borderland between Westmorland and Yorkshire on the watershed of the River Ure flowing south and the River Eden flowing north. Two mighty fells dominate the area, Wild Boar Fell and High Seat, each of about 2,230 feet (709m), while Pendragon Castle controlled the valley. This has legendary associations with Uther Pendragon, the father of King Arthur, but it was, in fact, built in the 12th century, and renovated in the mid-17th century by Lady Anne Clifford. It has long ago become impressively ruinous. Lady*

*Anne also restored Mallerstang Chapel at Outhgill which has recently acquired a beautiful set of hassocks made locally, each one depicting a scene from Mallerstang's history, landscape, wildlife and farming.*

**Marthwaite:** Morthwait 1235. ON maurr + ON thveit. The ant-infested clearing. Maurr can also be a personal name: Maurr's clearing.

**Millthrop:** Milnethorpe 1535. OE myln + ON thorp. The hamlet with the mills.

**Needle House:** Nedlehowse 1595. The home of the Needle or Nadler family.

**Outhgill:** Hothegill 1324. ON authr + ON gil. The desolate ravine.

*See note under Mallerstang.*

**Platt:** A plot of land. ME plat.

**Rash:** The Rashe 1592. Local dialect 'rash' = a strip of rocky ground in an arable field.

**Rawridding:** * OE raw + OE rydding. The clearing by a row of cottages or trees.

**River Rawthey:** Rautha 1224. ON rauthr + ON a. The red river.

*The river is a tributary of the Lune and has its source on Wild Boar Fell. It acquired its name from the red sandstone exposed along its course.*

**Raygill:** * ON ra + ON gil. The ravine frequented by roebucks.

*This remote spot in the upper reaches of Garsdale was the birthplace of John Dawson (1734-1820), eminent as a surgeon and mathematician in his day.*

**Riddings:** Riddenge 1287. OE rydding. The cleared land.

**Rise Hill:** Rysell 1771. OE hris + OE hyll. The hill covered with brushwood.

**Rivling:** * ME riveling. A rivulet.

**Rottenbutts:** * Probably derived from ON rotinn + ME butte, referring to the strips of soft ground on the boundary of a common field.

**Ruecrofts:** * Possibly OE ruh + OE croft. The enclosure with rough land.

**Sarthwaite:** * ON saurr + ON thveit. The clearing with sour or muddy land.

**Scales:** Scales 1137. ON skali. The shieling.

*'Skali' is a common element in areas of Norse settlement and is usually found with a second element. The shielings referred to were often on the seters or summer pastures in the uplands to which cows, sheep and goats were taken for the summer months. Butter and cheese were made on the seters and sent down to the valleys for sale or storage. This system of transhumance farming continued in Norway until the mid-20th century but was rarely found here after the Middle Ages.*

**Scotchergill:** The earliest recorded version of this name - Scotshellgill 1676 -

is rather late but an explanation based on this might be 'Scottr's ravine with the cave or recess'. ON personal name + ON hellir + ON gil.

**Sedbergh:** Setber 1086. ON set-berg. A hill with a flat or seat-shaped top.

*Sedbergh is the largest town in the Dales National Park. It achieved prominence in the 18th century when the turnpike roads from Kendal, Lancaster and Kirkby Stephen were constructed through the town. Coaching inns brought prosperity and this received a further boost with the establishment of a woollen, cotton and knitting industry in the following years. With a market charter dating from 1251 Sedbergh also gained from the agricultural expansion of the 19th century. In 1874 a wider fame was achieved when Sedbergh's 16th century grammar school joined the ranks of the public boarding schools. The original school building is now an elegant library and museum, rather more impressive than the site of the Norman motte and bailey castle which has no known history and no remains.*

**Settlebeck:** Settelbeck 1660. OE setl + ON bekkr. The stream by a dwelling house.

**Slack:** * ON slakki. A damp hollow.

**Smorthwaite:** Smeretwayt 1379. ON smjor + ON thveit. The clearing with rich (i.e. butter-producing) pasture

**Spice Gill:** Spitegill 1613. Spytr's ravine. The ON personal name, Spytr, was probably a by-name for someone who carried a spear-like stick (ON spjot) or an especially knobbly stick (ON spyta).

**Swarth Greaves:** * ON svatr/OE sweart + OE graefe. The dark copse.

**Taythes:** * Probably ON tatha/Dial tathe. A home-field with manure spread on it.

**Thorough Mea:** * Possibly OE thruh + OE maed. A meadow crossed by a drainage ditch.

**Thursgill:** Thursegile 1220. ON thurs + ON gil. The giant's ravine.

**Thwaite:** ON thveit. A clearing. 'Thwaite' is usually combined with a personal name or a term of description but these occasionally became lost as here. See also Thwaite in Swaledale.

**Tofts:** Tofts 1699. ON topt. An enclosure intended for a building. ('Toft' is in clear distinction to 'croft' which was a small enclosure for use as arable or pasture, often adjacent to a toft).

**Uldale:** Uldall 1656. ON ulfr + ON dalr. The valley frequented by wolves.

*The wolf was the most serious predator which threatened the medieval sheep farmer and it was not unusual for grants of land to be made with the*

*responsibility of keeping down the local wolf population. An English Book of Husbandry from the 13th century notes that shepherds had to guard their flocks by night as well as by day. The wolf became extinct in England during the 16th century.*

**Wham:**  Quane 13th c. OE whamm/ON hvammr. A marshy hollow or boggy land.

**Whins:**  * ON hvin. Land covered with gorse.

**Winder:**  Winderge 1193. ON vindr + ON erg. The windswept pastures.

*The steep but undemanding walk to the summit of Winder from Sedbergh is rewarded by a fine view over Dentdale, Garsdale, Lunesdale and Morecambe Bay.*

Near Clapham

**Ribblesdale:**   Rippel 710. OE ripel + ON dalr. The valley of the River
Ribble. The precise meaning of OE ripel in this name is obscure. Of the
various suggestions which have been put forward the most convincing is
probably an extension of one meaning of ripel - 'a strip of land' - to
indicate a boundary. The Ribble was the western boundary of the large
pre-Conquest district of Craven.

**Kingsdale:**   Kinesdale 1695. ME kyen (a plural form of 'cu') + OE dael. The
valley where cows were kept

*RIBBLESDALE and Kingsdale together form an area of caves, potholes, waterfalls and limestone scars, a fine example of the scenic effect of the action of ice, water and time. Trails based on Ingleton guide the visitor to some of the more accessible sites but these are just a few of the many which appear on the Ordnance Survey outdoor leisure map of this south-western corner of the National Park. The Three Peaks - Ingleborough, Whernside and Penyghent - dominate these two Dales, the last forming a definite barrier between Ribblesdale and Wharfedale and the first two firmly separating Ribblesdale from Kingsdale. There are few village settlements until the Kingsdale Beck and the Ribble approach the park boundary: this is, for the most part, a country of isolated farms following a pattern which has existed since the Norse settlers first came here 10 centuries ago. Only the lowland areas near Ingleton, Austwick and Settle reflect all the variety of rich limestone agriculture. It is here - and at Horton - that the hand of man has also been less in harmony with nature and the landscape has been scarred by quarry-working on a massive scale. But trade has been a feature of both Kingsdale and Ribblesdale for much of the last 2,000 years: Roman roads, monastic roads, packhorse routes, drove roads, turnpikes and the famous Settle to Carlisle railway have all been driven through these uncompromising dales, many of them now green lanes ideal for walking.*

**Alum Pot:** Allam Pott 1791. Possibly ON almr + ME potte. The deep hole by the elm tree. A number of potholes were identified in this way: e.g. Ash Pot and Hazel Pot near Ravenstonedale where an Elm Pot is recorded as Allm Pott in the 18th century. Larch Tree Hole, near Horton-in-Ribblesdale, is a more modern name.

*Alum Pot is a modest 200 feet (61m) deep but from a surface vantage point offers an awe-inspiring view of the rocks underground. It is three miles NW of Horton.*

**Apron full of Stones:** * This name, in common with The Devil's Apronful (near Appletreewick) and Sampson's Bratful (near Ennerdale), refers to a large unexcavated mound of stones which, according to popular legend, was inadvertently dumped there when the Devil tripped and spilled them out of the apron in which he was carrying them. All are probably burial mounds.

**Attermire:** Authulusmire 1160. ON personal name. Audulfr + ON myrr. Audulfr's marsh.

*Attermire Cave is part of a cave system a few miles to the east of Settle and, together with the Victoria Cave nearby, is among the most popular of all the caves in the Dales National Park. Equally impressive are the fine limestone crags of Attermire Scar above the cave.*

**Austwick:** Ousteuuic 1086. ON austr + OE wic. The dairy farm on the east side. 'East' may refer to the east side of Clapham.

**Bark House:** Barkehowse 1579. ON borkr + ON hus. The house where bark was stored.

*The bark of trees was used to produce the tannin solutions in which animal hides were soaked in the process of tanning leather. It was stored, after cutting from the trees, in bark houses some of which still survive.*

**Batty Moss:** The moss belonging to the Batty family. Local surname + ON mosi.

*This is the site of the great Ribblehead viaduct on the Settle-Carlisle Railway.*

**Beecroft:** * OE beo + OE croft. The small enclosure where bee-hives are kept.

**Beezleys:** This is probably 'the place to the east of the woodland clearing'. ON by + OE east + OE leah. Beezley is also a local surname.

*Nearby is Beezley Falls on the River Doe, one of the many waterfalls north of Ingleton.*

**Birkwith:** Bircwid 1189. ON birki + ON vithr. The birch wood

*Birkwith lies on the old packhorse route from Settle to Hawes and is in an area of well-known caves and potholes of which the most accessible are Calf Holes and Browgill Cave, Sell Gill Holes, Jackdaw Hole, and Penyghent Long Churn. All are dangerous and great care is necessary.*

**Blakamaya:** * Probably ON bleikr + Dial mea. The bleak pasture.

**Blea Moor:** Blemor 1293. ON bla + OE mor. The dark moor.

**Boggarts Roaring Holes:** The potholes where ghosts shriek. Boggart is a northern term for a ghost or goblin.

**Borrins:** * OE burgaesn. A cairn or burial mound. A common name found throughout the Dales and the Lake District.

**Brackenbottom:** Brakan bothom 1575. ON brakni + OE botm.The hollow where bracken grows.

**Braida Garth:** Bradagarth 1575. OE brad + ON a + ON garthr. The enclosure by the broad stream. The stream is the Kingsdale Beck.

**Broadrake:** Braidreke 1663. OE brad + ON rak (dial rake). The broad track where sheep and cattle are taken to the uplands. The track referred to is from the lowlands near Ingleton to Dent Head.

**Bruntscar:** Brundi-sker 1236. OE brende + ON sker. The rocky hillside cleared by burning.

**Cam:** Campe 1190. OE cam/ON kambr. The crest of a ridge.

*The name appears in Cam End and Cam Houses but the ridge itself is*

*along Cam Fell which carries an ancient track, once the Roman road from Ingleton to Bainbridge, then a busy packhorse route and coach road, and today a section of the Pennine Way. It is also the watershed dividing the Ribble and the Wharfe.*

**Carrs:**  * The marshes. ON kjarr.

**Castlebergh:**  * ME castel + OE beorg/ON borg. The hill with a fort. (The term 'castel' was often given to prehistoric encampments as well as to later forts. Antiquarian imagination often had an influence too).

**Catrigg Force:**  Catarige 1573. OE catt/ON katt + ON hyrggr (+ ON fors). The waterfall by wild-cat ridge.

*Catrigg Force is a pleasant waterfall on Stainforth Beck one mile from Stainforth.*

**Chapel-le-Dale:**  The chapel in the valley. This is a fairly modern version of the name of this hamlet. The french 'le' is even later than 1677 when the name is recorded as Chappall ith Dale, a convincing Yorkshire version. In earlier records the place appears as Ingleton Fells and the chapel as Fells Chapel; and the first known version describes it as 'Wisedale', the valley where the willows grow. OE withig + ON dalr.

**Clapham/Clapdale:**  Clapeham 1086/Clapedale 1190. OE claepe + OE ham or ON dalr. The homestead or valley with a noisy stream.

*Clapham is an excellent base from which to explore the limestone country just to the north of the village. A popular walk is the four-mile long Ingleborough Estate Trail which incorporates the original Farrer Nature Trail commemorating the well-known botanist Reginald Farrer whose family rebuilt Ingleborough Hall and transformed the landscape of much of Clapdale. They also opened up Ingleborough Cave which is now probably the best show-cave in the National Park. Clapham was the birthplace of Michael Faraday, the great electrical scientist who first identified the atom as the 'centre of force'.*

*Clapham is also the birthplace of the Dalesman Publishing Company, the most successful publishers of regional literature in Britain.*

**Cleatop:**  Clethop 1298. ON klettr + OE hop. The small valley under a cliff. Cleatop is in a recess in the steep hillside under Cleatop Park.

**Combe Scar:**  Colmes Hill 1847. ME colm + ON sker. The scar blackened as if with soot. 'Colm' is a northern dialect word for 'coal dust' or 'soot'.

**Crina Bottom:**  * OIr crin + OE botm. Dry valley bottom. It is also possible that the OIr personal name 'Crin' may form the first element. This place-name occurs twice within a short distance: once near White Scars at the foot of Ingleborough and again near Clapham.

**Crummackdale:** Crumbok 1190. Br crumbaco + ON dalr. The crooked valley.
*This remote little valley, two miles north of Austwick, is regarded as a gem of limestone scenery with shining white outcrops and cliffs, green landscapes and limestone pavements and unexpected traces of ancient settlements; all enhanced by the mysterious and crooked course of the Austwick Beck. It was from this valley that the glacier carried the huge gritstone boulders which now stand so prominently on the limestone hill of Norber Brow just to the south. (See Norber).*

**River Doe:** This is unexplained. The river was formerly known as the Wase which may, like Wasdale, be derived from ON vatn, water, or possibly from OE withig, willow: the valley is earlier referred to as Wisedale.

**Douk Cave:** (Great and Low): * The damp cave. Northern dialect douky = damp.

**Eller Beck:** * ON alor + ON bekkr. The alder stream.

**Feizor:** Fegesargh 1265. OIr/ON personal name, Fech + ON erg. Fech's upland pastures. Fech was a pre-Conquest landowner in these parts.

**Foredale:** * OE fore + OE dael. Foredale lies at the beginning of the upper part of Ribblesdale. In front of the valley.

**Gaping Gill:** * The chasm with a wide opening. ON gapa + ON gil.
*The 'gape' of Gaping Gill is 66 feet (20m) by 33 feet (10m) across and the depth is a sheer drop of 340 feet (104m). It is Britain's most spectacular pothole. The chamber below is as large as York Minster with an impressive cascade of water plunging all the way down to disappear into the floor and later to emerge in Ingleborough Cave. The first descent was made in 1895; it is now, for a brief period each summer, possible to descend by winch to view this remarkable sight.*

**Gauber:** Gober 1712. OE galga + OE beorg. Gallows Hill.
*Gauber lies near the junction of two ancient and well-used drove roads and packhorse routes and not far from the well-patronised Drovers' Inn at Gearstones. Lively gatherings here may well have led some to the gallows nearby.*

**Gearstones:** Gearston 1612. OE gara + OE stan. The stony triangular plot of land. This may refer to the land between the line of the Roman Road (probably marked by stones) and the Gayle Beck.

**Gearstones Inn:** - see Gauber.

**Giggleswick:** Ghigelswic 1086. OE personal name, Gikel + OE wic. Gikel's farm.
*Giggleswick has a fine church founded in the 12th century but now mainly*

*of the 15th century with much good 17th century woodwork. Many of the houses also date from the 17th century but the most prominent architectural feature is the famous public school with the copper dome of its late Victorian chapel dominating the town. The most distinguished building is Beck House, an outstanding 18th century residence.*

**Gragareth:**  Gragret 1307. ON grar + ON grjot. Grey stones.

*Gragareth just falls short of 2,000 feet (627m). A line of stones along its lonely ridge marked the frontier between Yorkshire and Westmorland. It is a somewhat dreary landscape but Gragareth has a claim to fame well hidden from those few who wander its desolate tracts. Beneath it lies the most extensive cave system in Britain. Over 33 miles of cave passages thread the western slopes and within the National Park on the eastern flanks are 7 miles more, with numerous waterfalls and many potholes including such well-known names as Jingling Pot, Rowten Pot and Yordas Cave.*

**Gunner Fleet:**  * ON personal name, Gunnar + ON fljot. Gunnar's stream.

**Harber:**  Haverbergh 1297. ON hafri + ON berg. The hillside where oats are grown.

**Haws House:**  Langhals 1190. ON langr + ON hals. The long pass over the mountains. The Roman Road from Bainbridge to Ingleton reaches the pass between Whernside and Ingleborough at this point. 'House' is a later addition.

**Hellifield:**  Haelgefeld 1086. ON personal name, Helgi + OE feld. Helgi's fields.

**Helwith Bridge:**  Helworthe Brigge 1590. ON hella + ON vath. ('Bridge' is a medieval addition). The ford made of flat stones.

*This ford and bridge across the Ribble are on an ancient and important route certainly used since early medieval times and probably before that. Travellers, merchants, packmen, drovers and the monks of Fountains Abbey all met at this crossing. Quarrymen from the nearby slate quarries also crossed here to transport the flat stones throughout Ribblesdale where they adorn cottage roofs, floors, porches, gateposts and form most of the headstones in the churchyards.*

**Holly Platt:**  Haly plat 1607. OE halig + ME plat. The holy plot of land.

*This small plot of land once belonged to the office of Proctor of Ingleton - an attorney in the Church Courts.*

**Horton-in-Ribblesdale:**  Hortune 1086. OE horu + OE tun. The farm on dirty land. 'Ribblesdale' is a 13th century addition to distinguish this Horton from Horton-in-Craven.

*Horton is a popular starting point for exploring Upper Ribblesdale. Its two inns have little difficulty in tempting weary walkers from the Pennine Way. The history of Horton is reflected in its houses: 17th century farmhouses, 18th century labourers' cottages, 19th century railwaymens' terraces and 20th century housing for the quarrymen who have created such great scars in the neighbouring landscape. Older than all these is St. Oswald's Church which still retains its fine Norman doorway and nave arcades, and its lychgates are roofed with Helwith flags.*

**Hull Pot:** * OE hulu + ME potte. The pot-hole by the shieling.

*Two miles north of Horton is the open chasm of Hull Pot, 300 feet long and 60 feet wide and 60 feet deep (91m x 18m x 18m), which after heavy rain has an impressive waterfall. Nearby is Hunt Pot, very much deeper (200 feet), but its opening is no more than a malevolent-looking slit in the fellside, a few inches wide and 15 feet long.*

**Ingleborough:** Ingelburh 1165. OE ing-hyll + OE burh. The fort on the hill.

*An Iron Age fort once covered much of the summit of Ingleborough and traces of its 1,000 yard-long (900m) enclosing wall may still be seen. Its height of 2,372 feet (723m) makes Ingleborough the second-highest of the Three Peaks.*

**Ingleton:** Ingelstune 1086. OE ing-hyll + OE tun. The farmstead by the hill.

*Once a staging post on the Roman Road from Bainbridge to Lancaster, Ingleton became an industrial town in the 18th and 19th centuries with woollen and cotton-spinning mills, coal mines and extensive quarries. Today it is a tourist centre, a base for the exploration of the many interesting features in the local limestone landscape. Most popular is the Ingleton Waterfalls Trail, a five mile walk visiting several falls and with a succession of geological and scenic surprises. A mile away are the White Scar Caves, a spectacular 'show-cave', with an array of waterfalls, stalagmites and stalagtites, open to the public from March to November.*

**Ivescar:** * OE ifig + ON sker. The scar covered in ivy.

**Jingling Pot:** The pothole with a tinkling, rattling noise. Dial. gingling + ME potte.

**Langcliffe:** Lanclif 1086. OE lang + OE clif. The long cliff.

**Ling Gill:** * ON lyng + ON gil. The ravine covered with heather.

*Ling Gill is a National Nature Reserve with a variety of plants and flowers some of which are now rarely seen; these include the giant bellflower, the globeflower, herb Paris and the melancholy thistle. The gill itself is a wooded limestone gorge and has a 16th century packhorse bridge (with a repair date 1765) which carried the ancient route from Settle to Hawes.*

**Long Preston:** Prestune 1086. OE preost + OE tun. The priest's farmstead. 'Long' was added to distinguish this settlement from the many other 'Prestons' and refers to its linear development.

**River Lune:** Loun 1094. No satisfactory explanation of this name has so far appeared. All suggestions raise serious etymological difficulties.

**Masongill:** Maising gile 1200. ON meisingr + ON gil. The ravine frequented by birds of the tit family

**Mearbeck:** * OE maere + ON bekkr. The stream marking a boundary. (A parish boundary).

**Moughton:** * OE muga + OE dun. The hill with a pile of stones (or a cairn).

**Neals Ing:** * OIr personal name, Nele + ON eng. Nele's meadow.

**Newby Head:** Neubi 1086. OE niwe + ON by. The highest part of the land in the manor of Newby. (OE heaford = 'head' often referred to land near the source of a river). The new farmstead.

*Furness Abbey owned the Manor of Newby (near Clapham) which included this piece of land in Ribblesdale.*

**Norber:** * OE/ON north + OE beorg/ON berg. The hill to the north (of Austwick?).

*Norber is well-known for the great boulders of Silurian gritstone deposited by the glacier on its way down Crummackdale. The limestone below them has eroded leaving these 'glacial erratics' stranded on pedestals.*

**Oxenber:** * OE oxa (gen. plural, oxna) + OE beorg. The hill where oxen pasture.

**Pecca Falls:** No explanation of this name has so far been discovered.

*These falls are on the Ingleton Waterfalls Trail.*

**Penyghent:** The full explanation of this name is unknown. The first element is Br penno = hill, the second is Br y = the (definite article); the final element 'ghent' has so far defied linguistic analysis. The most promising line of enquiry is that it may be related to the borderlands of the British Kingdom of Brigantia: 'Hill on the frontier'

*Penyghent at 2,277 feet (694m) is the lowest of the Three Peaks but makes up for this by the excellent views in all directions: the Howgill Fells, Wildboar Fell, Great Shunner Fell, Ingleborough, Pendle, Bowland, and the rolling hills of Wensleydale and Wharfedale. In the spring the slopes of Penyghent are bright with masses of purple and yellow saxifrage.*

**Rathmell:** Rodemele 1086. ON rauthr + ON melr. The red sandbank.

**Rayside:** OE ra + OE side. Roebuck hill.

**Rowten Pot:**  * OE hrutande + ME potte. The roaring pothole.

**Sannat Hall:**  Sandwath 13th c. OE sand/ON sandr + ON vath. Sandy ford.

> *Sannat Hall is near to a former ford across Tongue Gill on the ancient route from Wharfedale to Ingleton.*

**Scaleber:**  Skarlebergh 1651. ON skali + ON berg. The hill with a shieling.

**Scales:**  * ON skali. The shielings (upland huts). (See Scales in Dentdale).

> *Scales Moor above High Scales and Low Scales has some of the most impressive limestone pavements in the Dales.*

**Sell Gill:**  * ON sel + ON gil. The ravine with a shieling.

> *Sell Gill is an area of potholes including Sell Gill Holes right on the Pennine Way and with an underground chamber of immense proportions at 210 feet deep. Other potholes nearby are Jackdaw Hole, Penyghent Long Churn and Canal Cavern.*

**Selside:**  Selesete 1379. ON selja + ON sætr. The seter by the willow trees.

**Settle:**  Setel 1086. ON setl. A dwelling place.

> *Settle developed as a town following the construction of the Kendal-Keighley Turnpike in the mid-18th century and it has retained many of the handsome houses and inns of that period. The 'Settle Town Trail' is a useful guide to the many points of interest in a town which has been an important market centre for 750 years.*

**Silverdale:**  * OE seolfor + ON dalr. The silver valley. It seems very probable that the name is derived from the grey limestone which is so much a feature of the landscape. (cf Silverdale in Lancashire).

**Skir Beck:**  Skarbecke 1573. ON skirr or ON sker + ON bekkr. The bright stream or the stream on the scar. This stream rises on the scar nearby.

**Skirwith:**  Skyrhouth 1306. ON skirr + ON hofuth. The shining headland.

**Sleights:**  Slights. 1655. OE slaeget. The sheep pastures

**Smearsett:**  * ON smjor + ON sætr. The butter seter. A not uncommon reference to butter in place-names refers to the rich quality of the grass.

**Southerscales:**  Suterscales 1150. ON sutari + ON skali. The shoemaker's shieling.

> *Extensive limestone pavements may be seen at Southerscales.*

**Sowerthwaite:**  Sowretwaite 1597. OE sur + ON tveit. The clearing with sour soil.

**Stackhouse:**  Stacuse 1086. ON stakkr + ON hus. A house (barn) for stacking hay.

**Stainforth:**  Stainforde 1086. OE stan/ON steinn + OE ford. The stony ford.

*Stainforth on the east side of the Ribble was once known as Friar Stainforth as it was then the property of Sawley Abbey; Little Stainforth on the west side was known as Knight Stainforth, a reference to the baronets of the Tempest family. The ford linked the two places and in 1670 was replaced by the beautiful bridge which still spans the river and is protected by the National Trust.*

**Stockdale:** Stocadale 1160. OE stoc + OE dael. The valley with an outlying cattle farm.

**Storrs:** Askebaldstorths 1297. ON personal name, Askebald + ON storth. Askebald's woodland plantations.

**Studfold:** Stodefald 1379. OE stod-fold. An enclosure for horses.

*This was the property of the monks of Jervaulx Abbey who had a stud-farm here.*

**Sulber:** Solberc 1190. ON sol + ON berg. The sunny hill.

*Sulber is best-known for the long track eroded by both time and human feet into the limestone on the approach to Ingleborough from Horton-in-Ribblesdale. There is a theory that this may well have been originally created as an access route to the Iron Age fort on the summit.*

**Swarth Moor:** * OE swaert/ON svartr + OE/ON mor. The black moor.

**Taitlands:** Tadelandis 1280. OE tade + OE land. Land frequented by toads. A derivation from ON tatha, manured land, may also be possible.

**Thornton Force:** The waterfall in the parish of Thornton-in-Lonsdale (v below) + ON fors.

*At Thornton Force the River Twiss falls 46 feet (14m) over rocks which form an interesting geological structure. The cliff is clearly divided into two distinct sections: the upper a thick limestone band deposited in a shallow sea over 300 million years ago; the lower a vertical band of slates over 500 million years old. The pebbles and small boulders piled at the junction of these two layers are believed to represent the beach of an early sea.*

**Thorton-in-Lonsdale:** Tornetun 1086. OE/ON thorn + OE/ON tun. The farm among the thorns (in the valley of the Lune). Thortun-in-Lonesdale 1280.

**Trow Gill:** Trougill 1750. Doubtful: possibly ON troll or OE treow + ON gil. The troll's ravine or the ravine with trees.

*Trow Gill is a dry valley cut by the meltwater of a glacier. The river now flows underground, sinking in the chasm of Gaping Gill and emerging again in Ingleborough cave.*

**Turbary Pasture:** * ME turbarye. The land where turf is cut (for fuel).

*Rights of turbary were strictly controlled by customary procedures to ensure a fair distribution of what was often the main source of fuel.*

**River Twiss:** * OE twisla. The wedge of land formed by a river-fork. (See Twistleton.)

**Twistleton:** Thwisilton 1086. OE twisla + OE tun. The farmstead in a wedge of land formed by a river-fork. The River Twiss and the River Doe create a narrowing wedge of land as they flow towards their junction at Ingleton.

*Twistleton Scar is a good example of the action of a glacier in plucking away a rock face as it passes down a valley.*

**Wham:** Quane 13th c. OE hwamm/ON hvammr. A marshy hollow.

**Wharfe:** Warf 1224. ON hvarf. A corner of land. The reference is probably to the triangle of land between Austwick Gill and Wharfe Gill Sike. (The name is unrelated to the River Wharfe).

**Whernside:** Querneside 1202. OE cweorn + OE side. The hillside where querns (or millstones) were found.

*Whernside is the highest of the Three Peaks (2,419 feet/737m). Scales Moor on its southern slopes (above Twistleton Scar) has impressive limestone pavements.*

**Winshaw:** * OE hvin + OE sceaga. The gorse copse.

**Winskill:** Wyndescale 1414. ON vindr + ON skali. The windswept shieling.

**Winterscales:** * OE winter + ON skali. The shielings used in winter.

**Yordas Cave:** The origin of this name is unknown.

*Yordas Cave in Kingsdale is one of the most popular and accessible of the caves in the Dales National Park.*

**Airedale:** Eyr 1135. The origins of the river-name Aire are complex but seem to lie in the Greek word 'ieros' = 'strong' - from which is derived the Celtic river-name Isara and also the European rivers Isere, Isar and Oise. From Isara is derived the Celtic word Isa which became 'aia' in Old Welsh and 'air' or 'eger' in OE. The valley of the strong river.

Gordale Scar

*ONLY 3½ miles of the course of the River Aire lie within the Dales National Park but this short stretch is without doubt the most attractive of all. Here, from its source in the springs at Aire Head, the river flows through green fields, pleasant parkland and limestone villages with old cottages and reminders of a former spinning and weaving industry. The Pennine Way clings to the river bank all the way.*

**Malhamdale:** Malgum 1086. ON malr + ON dalr. The valley near the coves. The ON malr means literally 'shaped like a sack' and this is taken

57

to refer to the shape of Malham Cove. The ON 'i malhum' is the dative plural, meaning 'by or near the coves'.

*MALHAMDALE offers all that is best in spectacular limestone scenery: limestone pavements where rare and almost inaccessible plants are found; waterfalls and disappearing streams; potholes and awe-inspiring scars; a pattern of white limestone field-walls and green pastures; and wide sweeps of moorland broken by rocky outcrops. Here are the famous natural beauty spots of Malham Cove, Malham Tarn, Gordale Scar and Janet's Foss. Here, too, are the relics of the works of man - Celtic field systems, Norse and Angle settlements, medieval roads once the highways to Fountains Abbey, coal-mines, copper-mines and workings for calamine; and at Great Close the site of what was probably the country's largest cattle fair.*

**Airton:**  Ayrtone 1086. OE eger + OE tun. The farmstead by the River Aire.

*In the 18th and 19th centuries Airton was a busy industrial village with weaving and spinning mills along the River Aire. These have now been converted to other uses and together with the old cottages, with their dated lintels, grouped round the green, help to preserve the historical heritage of a pleasant village.*

**Bell Busk:**  Belbuske 1585. OE belle + ON buskr. The bell-shaped bush.

**Bordley:**  Bordelaie 1086. OE personal name, Brorda + OE leah. Brorda's clearing. OE brord = herbage is also possible.

*A small Bronze Age stone circle and traces of a Celtic field system may be seen on Malham Moor on the eastern side of Bordley.*

**Brockabank Laithe:**  Brocholeclif 1188. OE brocc-hol + OE clif (later OE banke) + ON hlatha. The barn near the bank with the badger sett.

*'Laithe' will be found in many place-names in the Dales indicating that the custom of building the isolated field barns which are so characteristic of Dales scenery originated with the Norse settlers. Each barn was intended to house four cows over the winter with sufficient hay stored in the loft above for this purpose. Many are now unused but farmers receive grants to maintain the structure in sound condition.*

**Calton:**  Caltun 1086. OE calf + OE tun. The farm where calves are kept.

**Capon Hall:**  Coupmanhowe 1457. ON kaupmann + ON haugr. The hill where the merchant lives or the merchant's hill.

*Capon Hall is situated by one of the major trading routes across the area, Mastiles Lane, which led from Nidderdale to Ingleton and beyond.*

**Cowper Cote:**  * OE coupare + OE cot. Cooper's cottage. This could refer to the surname Cooper or to the trade of a cooper.

**Crake Moor:** Crakemor 1303. ON kraka + OE mor. Crow moor.

**Craven:** Crafna 1160. Derivation uncertain but it could relate to the Celtic word 'craf' meaning garlic which would suggest 'the place where garlic grows'. The Domesday version 'Cravescire' indicates that Craven was already considered as a district, probably linked to a Norse Wapentake (a Norse territorial and administrative division).

**Crookrise:** Crokeris 1140. ON krokr + ON hris. The brushwood by the bend (in the valley).

**Darnbrook:** Dernebroc 1140. OE derne + OE broc. The hidden brook. This is the only example of an Anglo-Saxon 'brook' in the Dales where the Norse 'beck' is usual. There is also only one example in Westmorland - (Blackbrock, near Murton).

**Eastby:** Estby 1241. OE east + ON by. The farm on the east side (of the parish).

**Embsay:** Embesie 1086. OE personal name. Embe + OE haeg. Embe's enclosure. The word 'haeg' usually refers to a part of the forest enclosed for hunting.

*Embsay boasts two relics of the past: a small Bronze Age stone circle and a steam railway. The former is of no great interest; the latter runs for several miles and is based on restored Midland Railway stations.*

**Eshton:** Estune 1086. OE aesc + OE tun. The farmstead by the ash tree.

**Flasby:** Flatebi 1086. ON personal name, Flatr + ON by. Flatr's farmstead.

*Flasby is a pleasant hamlet sited away from modern roads and untroubled by tourist attractions, and so it has retained all the best characteristics of a Dales farming village. It has recently regained its Italianate Victorian mansion with its fine parkland which a public path enables all to enjoy. Nearby are the twin summits of Sharp Haw and Rough Haw with panoramic views across the heather moors and one of the best views of the Aire Gap.*

**Fornah Gill:** ffornagil hous 1457. ON personal name, Forni + ON gil. Forni's ravine. (House is a later addition.)

**Fountains Fell:** Fontance Fell 1540. OFr fontein + ON fjall. A property of Fountains Abbey.

*Perhaps the most interesting feature of the summit of Fountains Fell is the remarkable stone coke oven (now a protected monument) built in the early 19th century. Coal mined in the surrounding moorland was converted here into coke to be transported by packhorse to Malham where calamine (also mined nearby) was roasted for the manufacture of brass.*

*Fountains Abbey managed many of the farms in this area and held a number of granges.*

**Gargrave:** Geregrave 1086. OE gara/ON geiri + OE graef. The copse in a triangular plot of land.

**Gordale:** Gordale 12th c. ON gor + ON dalr. The dirty valley or the valley covered with manure. (Whether the state of the valley was related to the proximity of the cattle gathering ground at Great Close is open to speculation.)

*Gordale today is far from being a dirty valley. Gordale Beck flows through a beautiful dell and the waymarked walks from Malham to the scar via Little Gordale and Janet's Foss are among the best in the area. The scar is a spectacular ravine with limestone cliffs over 150 feet (45m) high, a fine illustration of the effects of wind and water.*

**Great Close:** * OE great + ME clos. The large enclosure.

*This is probably a late place-name originating with the droving trade in cattle. For this great field, 732 acres in extent still, was not only the site of what was perhaps the largest cattle fair in the country but was used regularly as a grazing and resting place for cattle on the move. In any one summer up to 20,000 cattle were grazed on this enclosure, and 5,000 were brought here for the fair.*

**Hanlith:** Hagnlith. ON personal name, Hagne + ON hlith. Hagne's hill slope.

**Hetton:** Hetun 1086. OE haeth + OE tun, The farm on the heathland.

**Ingle Bridge:** This may have the same derivation as Inghey Bridge which is just outside the National Park and is recorded in 1208 as Engwahe which means 'the ford by the meadow' - ON eng + ON vath.

**Kirkby Malham:** Chirchebi 1086, Kirkeby Malghum 1154. OE cirice/ON kirkju-byr. (See also Malham below). The village with a church.

*Kirkby is a common place-name in areas of Norse settlement and often a distinguishing name was added as in Kirkby Lonsdale, Kirkby Kendal, Kirkby Stephen, Kirkby Thore and Kirkby Malzeard.*

**Knowe Fell:** Knowle Fell 1664. OE cnoll + ON fjall. A hill top.

**Malham:** Malgum 1086. This is ON i malhum which is the dative of ON malr meaning literally 'shaped like a sack', no doubt referring to Malham Cove. The place near the cove.

*Malham and the countryside around it attract vast numbers of tourists each year. The limestone scenery here is some of the most spectacular in the country with, in addition, Malham Tarn and the Malham Field Centre, Janet's Foss waterfall, the fascination of water sinks and disappearing streams, and Malham Cove itself, an awe-inspiring amphitheatre with its 280 feet (85m) high cliff over which a massive waterfall once thundered. A National Park Trail leaflet guides the visitor to these and other points of interest in the area. Nor should the village of Malham be overlooked with its many attractive 18th century houses and farms in a sylvan setting.*

**Mastiles:**  Mastells 1626. OE mersc + OE stigel. The marshy track.

*Mastiles Lane runs from Kilnsey to Malham Tarn and is certainly marshy in some sections but the name is often given to a much longer route, for this ancient road extends well beyond the limits of Mastiles Lane. It was a Roman trans-Pennine road and passes through a Roman camp just east of Malham Tarn; it was the vital communications link between Fountains Abbey and its properties not only in the Dales but as far afield as the Lake District; it was also used as a trading route by merchants and packmen until the 19th century.*

**Orms Gill:**  Awmgill 1602. ON almr + ON gil. Elm tree ravine.

**Otterburn:**  Otreburne 1086. OE oter + OE burna. The otter stream.

*Few place-names refer to the otter which replaced the beaver as the river-huntsman's quarry and in Edward 1's reign an Act of Parliament was required to protect it.*

**Pikedaw:**  Pykethow 1269. OE piced + ON haugr. The pointed hilltop.

*Pikedaw Hill to the west of Malham village is a splendid viewpoint over the Malhamdale scenery including the Cove, the Tarn, the field patterns and the limestone landscape. Two hundred years ago the mine workings near the summit were the source of many tons of zinc carbonate or calamine, a mineral used in the manufacture of brass. The calamine was processed at the early 17th century Calamine House, in Malham, by the Cheadle Brass Company. Nearby Nappa Cross is a restored medieval cross and also a magnificent viewpoint.*

**Scosthrop:**  Scotthorp 1225. ON personal name, Skottr + ON thorp. Skottr's outlying farm or hamlet.

**Skipton:**  Scipetone 1086. OE sceap + OE tun. The sheep farm. Norse influence changed the softer 'Shipton' into the harder 'Skipton'.

*Skipton was first settled by Anglian sheep farmers in the 7th century but it quickly developed into prominence after the Norman Conquest. Its position in the strategic Aire Gap made it an ideal site for a stronghold and in the 12th century Skipton Castle dominated the many routes which converge at this point. Much of the castle we see today is the result of the restoration carried out by Lady Anne Clifford in the 17th century although some Norman and medieval work still remains. It is the most complete 'medieval' castle in England. Skipton's Holy Trinity church is largely 14th century work reflecting the town's years of prosperity as a market for a very wide area. During the 18th century the main turnpike road and later the Leeds-Liverpool Canal gave Skipton a new importance; first woollen mills and then cotton-spinning mills transformed a small market town with a population of only a few thousands into an industrial centre of (by the late 19th century) more than 13,000 people. Skipton is still a busy place but it is now fortunately by-passed by all the traffic routes which meet there. The Craven Museum in the Town Hall tells the story of the whole area.*

**Sleets:** Slights 1655. OE slaeget. Sheep pastures.

**Stirton:** Stratton 1120. OE straet + OE tun. The farmstead by the road.

*Stirton is by the old road from Kendal to Skipton.*

**Thoragill:** Thirnegyll 13th c. OE thyrne + ON gil. The thorny ravine.

**Thorlby:** Toreilderebi 1086. ON personal name + ON by. Thoroldr's farmstead.

**Trenhouse:** Tranehouse 1416. ON personal name + ON hus. Trani's house. ON trani meaning 'a crane' is possible but seems improbable when associated with 'house'.

**Watlowes:** * Etymology obscure. No satisfactory explanation of this name has been suggested.

**Winterburn:** Wynterburn 1155. OE winter + OE burn. The stream which flows only in the winter months.

# WHARFEDALE WITH LITTONDALE AND LANGSTROTHDALE

## Wharfedale:

Hwerverdale 1180. OE weorf or ON hverfr. The valley of the winding river. The River Wharfe probably derives its name, like other Dales rivers, from a Celtic word (uerb?) but it is more obviously derived from OE weorf or ON hverfr, both of which mean 'winding'. Weorf 963/Werf 1158 .

Near Hubberholme

*MOST of the 30 miles of Wharfedale from Ilkley to the source of the river on Cam Fell present a pleasantly wooded scene with green, walled pastures threaded by tumbling becks cascading down from uplands adorned by grazing sheep and the white limestone scars. The Great Scar Limestone dominates the whole valley, sometimes in long hillside cliffs, sometimes in natural rock-garden outcrops, often in small waterfalls or cascades, occasionally with dramatic effect as at the spectacular Kilnsey Crag. The long history of man in Wharfedale is revealed in several Bronze Age stone circles, in a Roman road down the valley to Ilkley, in Anglian village settlements in the*

63

*lower valley and Norse hamlets in the upper. Langstrothdale Chase, Bolton Priory, Barden Tower and Hubberholme Church remind us of the Norman barons and their hunting forests, the great age of monasticism, the long arm of the Clifford family and the quiet dignity of ordinary Dalesfolk in their Christian faith. The rectangular fields enclosed by endless miles of drystone walls date from little more than 200 years ago when the Enclosure Acts brought the medieval common fields to an end and changed the face of English agriculture. Few traces are left of Wharfedale's cottage textile industry or of the many corn mills but the scars of the Duke of Devonshire's lead mines still remain on Yarnbury Moor. Of all the works of man in Wharfedale perhaps the most notable and charming are the beautifully built and carefully preserved stone houses, cottages, farmsteads and barns, a wealth of fine 17th century architecture, none of it very far from the banks of the Wharfe, the winding river.*

**Langstrothdale:** Langestrode 1190. OE lang + OE strother + OE dael/ON dalr. The valley with a long stretch of marsh overgrown with brushwood.

*THE Normans created a hunting forest out of Langstrothdale, and the inhabitants of the Norse settlements within its bounds - Beckermonds, Cray, Hubberholme, Oughtershaw, Raisgill and Yockenthwaite - became subject to the severe Forest Laws of the time. Today new forests of conifers have appeared in the upper reaches, ironically in areas which 200 years ago were the scene of agricultural experiments which earned the praise of Arthur Young. At Beckermonds the valley road divides - the western road following an ancient packhorse route between Richmond and Lancaster, the northern climbing over Fleet Moss and crossing the Roman road which ran from Bainbridge to Lancaster, and so on to Wensleydale.*

**Littondale:** Littunedale 12th c. ON hlith + OE/ON tun + ON dalr. The valley with the farm on a hill slope. (Littondale takes its name from the village of Litton and not from the river which flows through it - the Skirfare).

*LITTONDALE is a valley of limestone scenery and rich green pastures, quite unspoiled by mining. It was once farmed by Fountains Abbey which reared cattle and sheep here and also cultivated crops of corn. Many of the fine barns to be seen along the valley had stone threshing floors, some of which still remain. Littondale has a conspicuous literary history: Charles Kingsley named it Vendale, Wordsworth called it Amerdale and it is now popularly famous as Emmerdale*

**Addingham:**  Haddincham 1180. OE personal name + OE ing-ham. Adda's farmstead.

*Addingham was the birthplace of Samuel Cunliffe Lister (1815-1906) the inventor of over 150 mechanical processes for the textile industry. His most renowned achievement was to develop a machine for the worsted industry which could handle the very complex combing operation. This laid the foundations of his own fortune and of the prosperity of the city of Bradford and of the Australian woollen trade. He gave Lister Park to the citizens of Bradford.*

**Amerdale Dub:**  * The pool in the valley frequented by buntings. There are no early recorded forms of this name and this interpretation is suggested on the basis of a derivation from OE amore = bunting + ON dalr + OE dub.

**Appletreewick:**  Apletrewic 1086. OE aeppel-treow + OE wic. The farm by the apple tree.

*Appletreewick, pronounced 'Aptrick', became a prosperous settlement in 1300 when it was acquired by Bolton Priory which established an important grange here on the site of what is now the 17th century house known as Monk's Hall. High Hall was the home of Sir William Craven who became Lord Mayor of London in the early years of the 17th century when he also founded Burnsall Grammar School. Between High Hall and Low Hall at the bottom of the hill, are many attractive stone houses including Mock Beggar Hall, a name usually given to houses notorious for their parsimonious attitude to charitable causes. Appletreewick's market, granted in the 14th century, flourished until the late 19th century.*

**Arncliffe:**  Arneclife 1086. OE earn + OE clif. The eagles' cliff.

*Arncliffe is the largest settlement in Littondale and is an attractive village with its stone houses, farms and barns set round a spacious green. The yeoman's house, known as Old Cotes, bears the date 1650 on its two-storey porch.*

**Barben Beck:**  * ON bjorr + ON brunnr (+ ON bekkr). The beaver stream. See note on Barbon in Dentdale.

**Barden:**  Berdene 1140. OE bere + OE denu. The valley where barley is grown.

*In a beautiful setting near the River Wharfe, Barden Tower is a ruined medieval hunting lodge restored in the mid-17th century by the ubiquitous Lady Anne Clifford. Chapel House nearby was a priest's house probably built in the 15th century. A particularly fine example of a Dales 'bunkbarn' is close by.*

**Beamsley:**  Bedmeslei 1086. OE personal name, Bedhelm + OE leah. Bedhelm's clearing.

*Beamsley has a late Tudor Hospital (restored by Lady Anne Clifford in 1650) notable for its unusual circular Chapel. Better known, perhaps, is Beamsley Beacon, a famous viewpoint at almost 1,300 feet (393m), one of a chain of ancient beacons and last prepared for use at the time of the threatened Napoleonic invasion in 1803.*

**Beckermonds:** Beckermotes 1241. ON bekkr + ON mot. The place where the streams meet. Two becks, Oughtershaw Beck and Greenfield Beck, meet here to form the River Wharfe.

**Bolton Abbey:** Bodeltone 1086. OE bothl-tun. The enclosure with dwellings, a hamlet.

*The name 'Abbey' does not appear until some time after the Dissolution and refers more accurately to the priory of the Augustinian canons founded in 1155. The name is recorded in 1445 as 'Bolton-de-Chanons'. The ruins have a special beauty and were painted by both Turner and Landseer; the nave of the priory remains as the parish church and has a fine 13th century west front. The priory gatehouse is preserved nearby in Bolton Hall and also not far away is a very fine tithe barn. Public footpaths and nature trails through Bolton woods and the surrounding parkland make this a popular place for visitors.*

**Brass Castle:** * There are six 'Brass Castles' in Yorkshire and the name is thought to be an ironically pretentious description of a farm on very poor soil, there being little money or 'brass' to be made there.

**Brearlands:** * OE brerig + OE land. The land covered with briars.

**Buckden:** Buckedene 1235. OE bucc + OE denu. The valley frequented by bucks.

*Buckden was developed as a thriving settlement in the 12th century following the establishment of Langstrothdale Chase as a Norman hunting forest. A section of the Roman road through Wharfedale runs from the village to Cray well above the modern road. Buckden Pike, 2,302 feet (713m), is one of the highest peaks in the National Park, some 70 feet lower than Ingleborough but 25 feet higher than Penyghent.*

**Burnsall:** Brineshal 1086. OE personal name, Bruni or Bryni + OE halh. Bruni's nook of land in the river bend.

*The geology of Wharfedale changes at Burnsall: the limestone scars and field-walls of the upper valley are replaced by the darker moorlands and walls of gritstone country. The village has a number of fine stone houses of the 17th and 18th century and Sir William Craven's grammar school founded in 1602, a building worthy of the local man who became Lord Mayor of London. Nearby is St. Wilfrid's church with some 14th century work, a Norman font, two Anglian crosses and two Viking hog-back tombstones. The lych-gate is one of the unusual tapsell or turnstile gates.*

**Capplestones:** * ON kapall + ON steinn. The stony place where horses gather: cf Deerstones, Kidstones, etc.

**Clowder:** * OE cluder. A mass of rocks or rubble.

**Conistone:** Cunestune 1086/Cunigstun 1180. OE cyning/ON kunung + OE/ON tun. The king's farm.

*Anglian field systems and strip lynchets and evidence of a pre-Conquest church indicate that Conistone was a well-established settlement long before the arrival of the Normans in this part of the country. The village is well-endowed with 17th century houses and barns, mostly well-preserved. The nearby gorge known as Conistone Dib enjoys some splendid limestone scenery.*

**Cosh:** Grenfeld coche 1457/The Coshe 1496. ME cosh + OE grene + OE feld. The hut in the green open pastures.

**Cracoe:** Crakehow 1175. ON kraka + ON haugr. Crow hill.

**Cray:** Crei 1241. A Celtic river-name from Old Welsh 'crei'. The fresh river. (The name Creigate recorded in 1202 is probably a reference to the nearby Roman road through Wharfedale, the full route of which has yet to be traced.)

**Deerstones:** Dyrstonnes 1381. OE deor + OE stan. The stony place where deer gather.

**Devil's Apronful:** * See 'Apron full of Stones' in Kingsdale (page 47).

**Dibble's Bridge/River Dibb:** * OE dybb = a pool (often referring to a stream).

**Douky Bottom Cave:** * Dial douky + OE botm. The damp cave in the hollow: cf Great and Low Douk Caves in Ribblesdale (page 50).

**Drebley:** Drebelaie 1086. OE personal name, Drebba + OE leah. Drebba's clearing.

**Elbolton:** * ON elri + OE bothl-tun. The village among the alder trees.

*Alder wood was once widely used for making clogs, water troughs and spinning wheels, and for a black dye for dyeing coarse cloths.*

**Eller Beck:** * ON elri + ON bekkr. The stream among the alder trees.

**Eshber:** * OE aesc + OE beorg. Ash-tree hill.

**Flask:** Flaskes 1251. ON flask. Boggy ground.

**Fleets:** * OE fleot/ON fljot. By the streams. (There are numerous becks nearby).

**Foxup:** Foxhope 1457. OE fox + OE hop. The valley frequented by foxes.

**Garrellgum:** Garum gil 1812. No explanation of this name has been suggested.

**Ghaistrill's Strid:** Ghaistrill is a surname. OE stride = a narrow channel.

**Grassington:** Ghersintone 1086. OE gaersing + OE tun. The farm among the pastures.

*Grassington's situation made it an important crossroads from all points of the compass. Monks from Fountains and Byland, wool traders and packmen, miners and millworkers, travellers by horse and stagecoach, and modern visitors by rail and road, all came to and through Grassington. Extensive relics of the Duke of Devonshire's lead mines remain on the moors above the town but of greater interest to most visitors are the many fine 17th and 18th century houses and other buildings all within a few minutes walk of the cobbled town square. An informative trail guide is available. Grass Woods, one mile north of Grassington, is a notable nature reserve with over 400 plant species. Despite its historical importance Grassington has no Anglican church: this is at Linton across the river.*

**Grimwith:** Grymwith 1540. OE grima + ON vithr. The wood haunted by a ghost or goblin.

**Halton East:** Haltone 1086. OE halh + OE tun. The farm in a nook of land. ('East' is to distinguish this village from West Halton).

**Halton Gill:** Haltongyll 1457. OE halh + OE tun + ON Gil. The farm in a nook of land by a ravine.

*Halton Gill is at the head of Littondale and is one of the most attractive hamlets in the Dales with its 17th century houses grouped round a pleasant green.*

**Hartlington:** Hertlintone 1086/Hertlyngton 1198. OE personal name, Heortla + OE ingatun. The farm belonging to Heortla's people.

*The Hartlingtons were an important family in Wharfedale in the Middle Ages and had their 'seat' at Hartlington Hall set in woodland above Barben Beck which powered a corn mill nearby. The present Hall dates from 1894.*

**Hawkswick:** Hochesuuic 1086/Houkerswyk 1226. ON personal name, Haukr + OE wic. Haukr's farm.

**Hebden:** Hebedene 1086. OE heope + OE denu. The valley where wild roses grow.

**Henstone Band:** * OE henn + OE stan + Dial band. 'The stony ridge where wild birds gather' is a possible interpretation here.

**Hesleden:** Eseldene 1206. OE haesel + OE denu. The valley where hazel trees grow.

**Hubberholme:** Hubergheha 1086/Hulberham 1220. OE personal name,

Hunberg + OE ham. Hunberg's homestead. The early forms of this name show that it is not an ON 'holmr' name but an OE 'ham' name. It is pronounced 'Hubberham'.

*Hubberholme stands at the entrance to Langstrothdale in a beautiful setting on the River Wharfe. Its 12th century church, originally a forest chapel, is renowned for its rare 16th century rood-loft and its carved woodwork from four centuries, the 20th century represented by the work of Robert Thompson of Kilburn whose famous 'mouse' trademark appears on the pews and chairs. On every New Year's Eve the 'Hubberholme Parliament' meets in the George Inn (formerly the vicarage) when the vicar supervises the auction of the grazing rights of a field known as 'The Poor Pasture', a custom now at least 1,000 years old. An old packhorse bridge over Crook Gill, half a mile away, is on the ancient route from Bishopdale to Wharfedale.*

**Ilkley:** There is little doubt that this was the Roman town of Olicana as recorded by Ptolemy in 150 but the exact meaning of the name is unclear. It is recorded as 'Hillicleg' in 972 and as 'Illiclei' in 1086 and if the final element indictates OE 'leah', a possible explanation might be 'The forest clearing near the fort of Olicana'.

*Little remains of Roman Olicana but Ilkley retains much of its former elegance as a leading spa town when middle-class gentry flocked here to take the waters. The White Wells Springs were well patronised from the 1840s but it was the Ben Rhydding hydropath which made Ilkley famous with its pioneering methods in hydrotherapy. Ilkley Moor is, of course, universally known in the popular ballad but the area is also notable for its Bronze Age rock-carvings, particularly the so-called 'Swastika Stone' and the 'Cup and Ring Carvings'. In the town All Saints church has several Saxon crosses in the churchyard. The Wharfe here is crossed by an elegant bridge from 1673, now closed to traffic.*

**Kail Hill:** Calesleightes 1627. ON kal + ON sletta. The cabbage field.

**Kettlewell:** Cheteleuuelle 1086. OE cetel/ON ketill + OE wella. The bubbling spring.

*Kettlewell flourished in medieval times when Fountains Abbey, Bolton Priory and Coverham Abbey all held estates here. A market established in the 13th century and brought further prosperity to the village. In more recent centuries the cottage textile industry and lead mining and smelting ensured continued vitality - sufficient, in fact, to provide a livelihood for three inns in this small community. Many fine 17th and 18th century houses are also witness to Kettlewell's thriving economy. Its superb natural setting and the many excellent walks available from the village have secured its position as a mecca for tourists.*

**Kidhaw Gate:** * ON kith + ON haugr + ON gata. The hill where young goats gather near the (Roman) road.

*Kidhaw Gate is at the summit of the Roman road from Bainbridge and marks an important watershed. The Ribble flowing to the Irish Sea has its source nearby as does the Wharfe flowing to the Humber and the North Sea.*

**Kilnsey:** Kylnesey 1146. This may be either OE personal name, Cynel + OE eg - 'Cynel's water meadow', or OE cyln + OE saega - the marsh by the kiln. The former seems more likely as lime-burning in kilns was not practised as early as the 12th century.

*Kilnsey's chief claim to fame is its spectacular scar, a massive limestone cliff 170 feet high and with a 40ft overhang where an ice-age glacier cut away the rock. Rock-climbers find the challenge of this crag irresistible but more earthbound folk take their pleasure in the various facilities for refreshment and enjoyment in the visitor centre at Kilnsey Park. The 17th century house known as Old Hall stands on the site of a grange of Fountains Abbey and marks the beginning of Mastiles Lane, the line of communication between the abbey and its estates in Yorkshire and beyond.*

**Kirk Gill:** Kirkegill 1499. ON kirkja + ON gil. The ravine near the Church. Gill Beck in Kirk Gill joins the Wharfe opposite Hubberholme Church.

**Knipe Scar:** Gnip 1176. ON gnipa + ON sker. A steep rocky outcrop.

**Lainger House:** Langer hous 1416. OE lengan/ON lengja + ON hus. A house in which to rest for a time. This may have been a hospice belonging to Fountains Abbey.

**Langbar:** Langberh 1199. OE lang + OE beorg. The long hill.

**Laund:** * ME launde. A forest glade, a grassy place in the forest.

**Linton:** Lynton 1150. OE lin + OE tun. The farm where flax is grown.

*Linton is regarded by many as the most attractive of all the Dales villages. Linton Beck flows across the spacious green which is surrounded by groups of 17th and 18th century houses and, on one side, is dominated by the splendid edifice of Fountaine Hospital, founded in 1721 for 'six poor men or women' and designed in the style of (and possibly by) Sir John Vanbrugh, the architect of Castle Howard. Linton's bridges are noteworthy: the beck is crossed here by a packhorse bridge, a clapper bridge, a modern road bridge and by Little Emily's Bridge. There are also stepping stones for variety. Linton's woollen mill has long vanished but the 12th century Church of St. Michael's remains and still serves the people of Grassington, Hebden, Threshfield and Linton.*

**Litton:** Litone 1086. ON hlith + OE tun. The farm on the hill slope.

*The village of Litton gives its name to Littondale (see page 64). Fine examples of the best in architectural design, both old and new, may be seen in Litton: the former in the older building whose roof-lines so closely reflect the angle of the hillside, and the latter in the sensitive conversions of several of the splendid old barns for which Littondale is renowned. Footpaths following the River Skirfare link the settlements of Foxup, Halton Gill, Litton, Arncliffe and Hawkswick, and provide an excellent way to explore this delightful valley.*

**Nussey House:** Nussehouse 1540. The home of the Nussey family.

**Old Cote:** Ulecotes 1246. OE ule + OE cot. The cottage haunted by owls.

**Oughtershaw:** Uhtredescal 1241. OE personal name, Uhtred + OE sceaga. Uhtred's wood.

**Pace Gate:** * Possibly ME pas + ON gata. The road through the pass. (The road from Skipton goes through the hills along Kex Beck at this point).

**Parcevall Hall:** Percevell Hall 1667. The Percival family lived here in the 17th century.

*The Hall is now an Anglican retreat but its grounds and terraced gardens are open to the public.*

**Pinder Stile:** * ME pindere + OE stigel. The pinder's path.

*A pinder was an officer of the medieval manor whose duty was to round up and impound stray animals.*

**Posforth Gill:** Poseford 1180. ON personal name, Posi + OE ford. Posi's ford (+ ON gil).

*This area was struck by a violent storm in the early 19th century and has since been known as the Valley of Desolation.*

**Rainscar:** Raynscar 1409. ON hrafni + ON sker. Raven scar.

**Raisgill:** Reisegill 1241. ON hreysi + ON gil. The ravine with a cairn or pile of stones.

**Ranelands:** This is probably 'the strip of land along the boundary of the common field'. OE ran/ON rein + OE land.

**Rylestone:** Rilestune 1086. OE rille + OE tun. The farmstead by the stream.

**Scoska:** Coscoe 1837. The second element seems to be ON skogr but there is no other clue to the meaning of the name as a whole.

**River Skirfare:** Chiphare 1170. ON skirr + ON fara. The bright, clear river.

*The Skirfare is the river which flows down Littondale to join the Wharfe at Amerdale Dub, just north of Kilnsey Crag.*

**Skirethorns / Skythorns:** Skyrthornes 1567. ON skirr + ON thorn. The bright thorn bushes

**Skyreholme:** Skerome 1540. ON skirr + ON holmr. The bright water-meadow.

**Spittle Croft:** Spittlecroft 1585. ME spital + OE croft. The small enclosure with a hospital. (Hospitals or hospices were usually associated with a religious foundation).

**Starbotton:** Staverbotten 1330. ON stafn + ON botn. The valley bottom where stakes are cut.

**Storiths:** Le Storthes 1214. ON storth. The plantations.

**Strans:** * OE strand. Land at the water's edge (in this case the bank of the River Wharfe).

**The Strid:** This literally means 'the striding place' (OE stride) and refers to a narrow channel where the River Wharfe has worn down through the rock to a depth of 30 feet. The Strid 1817.

*Many have been tempted to 'stride' or jump over this channel, some with fatal results. Wiser folk enjoy the surrounding woods, perhaps following a Nature Trail described as 'One of the most romantically beautiful woodland and riverside walks in England'.*

**Stump Cross:** Cruce supra Botton 1205. ON stumpr + OE cros. The broken cross.

*Stump Cross was probably an early Christian preaching place but it is now famous for its extensive cave system with fine displays of stalactites and stalagmites. The cave is open to the public and is excellently interpreted with good lighting and an interesting video presentation. It was discovered by lead miners in 1858, but long before that it was home to wolverine, bison and reindeer.*

**Summerscales:** * ON sumarr + ON skali. The shieling used in the summer months. This probably refers to a seter.

**Thorpe:** Torp 1086. ON thorp. An outlying farm or small hamlet.

**Threapland:** Threppelandes 1200. OE threap + OE land. The land over which ownership is disputed.

**Threshfield:** Treskefeld 1192/Threscefeld 1256. OE thresc-feld. Open land where threshing takes place.

*Houses from the mid-17th century cluster round the green at Threshfield. The manor house is particularly interesting with its three-storey porch and rose window, and close by is a fine three-door barn of the same period. The 14th century Old Hall is now behind the Old Hall Inn, a 19th century coaching inn. Standing in isolation, half a mile away, is the former*

*Threshfield Grammar School, founded in 1674 and still in use as a primary school.*

**Trollers Gill:** * ON trol + OE aers + ON gill. The giant's arse ravine.Trolls were giants in Scandinavian mythology.

*Trollers Gill is a great cleft in the hills, a very rough and atmospheric gorge full of tumbled rocks from which streams emerge from underground. It is narrow and damp, not a place for the squeamish but of great interest to the botanist. A permissive 'route' goes through it but no path exists.*

**Trunla Gill:** * OE trun + OE leah + ON gil. The ravine with a circular clearing.

**The Whams:** * OE hwamm/ON hvammr/Dial wham. The marshy hollows.

**Whinhaugh:** * ON hvin + ON haugr. The gorse-covered hill.

**Windle Side:** * OE wind + OE hyll + OE side. The windswept hillside.

**Yarnbury:** No early form of this name is available but as there is an ancient Bronze Age henge nearby (a prehistoric circle of the type which later ages believed to have been fortified encampments), it is probable that it is derived from an OE personal name Earn + OE burh. Earn's fort.

**Yockenthwaite:** Yoghannesthweit 1241. ON personal name, Eoghan or Yoghan + ON thveit. Eoghan's clearing.

*Yockenthwaite is a pretty riverside hamlet, the last wooded settlement before the more austere moorlands of Langstrothdale. There is a single-arch bridge over the Wharfe which carried the old packhorse route between Settle and Wensleydale. Just up-river from this bridge is the best prehistoric stone circle in the Dales with 20 stones still in place forming a circle 25 feet (7.6m) in diameter.*

Nidderdale from Middlesmoor

**Nidderdale:** Nid 715/Nide stream 890. 'Nidd' is a Celtic river-name of obscure origin but probably related to the Latin word 'nideo' and the old Irish 'niamde' meaning 'brilliant' or 'bright'. With ON dalr the whole name would therefore mean 'the valley of the bright river'.

*NIDDERDALE is not included within the boundaries of the Yorkshire Dales National Park for a number of reasons and it has not, therefore, enjoyed the standard of management associated with our National Parks. Even so, Nidderdale is an area of largely unspoilt natural beauty with its sparkling river, its charming villages and its spacious moorland views. The construction of three reservoirs in the early decades of the 20th century has given Nidderdale the attraction of fine stretches of open water which are notably lacking in the other Dales. The medieval monastic foundations of Fountains and Byland abbeys developed the dairy and sheep farming of the valley and exploited the deposits*

74

*of lead and iron, while later ages quarried the flagstones and established a thriving flax industry. Industrial development was not accompanied, until recent years, by significant change in the traditional way of life in Nidderdale. Many old customs and even many old words survived here much longer than elsewhere.*

**Angram:** Angrum 1276. 'Angrum' is the dative plural of OE anger = pasture. By the pastures.

*Angram Reservoir is one of three reservoirs built in Nidderdale in the first half of the 20th century to supply water to the City of Bradford. The others are Scar House Reservoir and Gouthwaite Reservoir. The Nidderdale Light Railway was built to facilitate the construction of these 'lakes' which are a special feature of the Nidderdale landscape. All are well-known to bird-watchers.*

**Armathwaite:** Armenthwaite 1771. ME personal name, Ermina + ON thveit. Ermina's clearing.

**Arnagill:** * Possibly ON personal name, Arni + ON gil. Arni's ravine.

**Ashfold Gill:** Eskefald 1270. OE aesc + OE fald + ON gil. The ravine with a sheepfold by an ash-tree.

*Ashfold Gill was mined for lead for probably 2,000 years; first by the Celtic Brigantes, then by the Romans, later by the monks of Byland Abbey, and finally by modern industrialists. The last lead was mined in 1889.*

**Autherlands:** Aldolflund 1314. ON personal name, Aldulfr + ON lundr. Aldulfr's grove.

**Aygill/Agill:** * Possibly ON a + ON gil. The ravine with a stream.

**Backstone Gill:** Bakestone Gill 1817. OE baec-stan + ON gil. The ravine where bakestones are found.

*Bakestones were large flat stones on which the traditional north-country thin oat bread (or clapbread) was baked. This type of bread, still widely used in Scandinavia, was brought by the Norsemen and was baked in every kitchen until modern times.*

**Banger House:** Brangerhouse 1458. ME personal name, Beringar + ON hus. Beringar's house.

**Bewerley:** Beurlie 1086. OE beofor + OE leah. The woodland glade frequented by beavers.

*One of the uncommon 'beaver' names - see Barbon in the Dentdale section. The manor of Bewerley was a property of Fountains Abbey, an important grange and a source of revenue from the lead mines at Greenhow. The monks' chapel at Bewerley, now restored, still bears Abbot Huby's motto 'Soli Deo Honi et Gloria'. Bewerley Hall was the home of the Yorke family; it was demolished in 1928.*

**Birstwith:** Beristade 1086. This is probably OE byre + OE stede - the site of a cowshed; but ON byjar-stathr, a village, is also possible.

**Bishopside:** Byshopsyd 1459. OE biscop + OE side. The bishop's hill. *This was part of the Archbishop of York's manor of Ripon.*

**Blayshaw:** Le Blashagh 1346. ON blar + OE sceaga. The dark wood.

**Blazefield:** * Probably ON blesi + OE feld. A bleak tract of open land.

**Blubberhouses:** Bluberhusum 1172. ME bluber + ON husum. The houses by the bubbling springs.

**Bouthwaite:** Burtheit 1184. ON bur + ON thveit. The clearing with a storehouse.

**Braithwaite:** Bradewath 1283. OE brad/ON breidr + ON vath. The broad ford.

**Brandrith:** * This is probably OE brand + ON ryth. The clearing made by burning. It seems unlikely, but not impossible, that the derivation could be ON brand-reith which indicates a beacon-fire as at Brandreth near Great Gable in the Lake District.

**Brandstone Beck:** Branston Gill 1858. ON brant + ON steinn + ON gil. The steep stony ravine.

**Breaks Fold:** Breakes Sheephouse 1613. OE breac + OE fald. The fold by a thicket.

**Brimham:** Bernebeam 1135. OE personal name, Byrna + OE beam. Byrna's tree.

*Brimham Hall was a grange of Fountains Abbey. Its nearby lodge, Brimham Lodge, is a fine surviving example of a three-storey Nidderdale house.*

*Brimham Rocks, a National Trust property, are unique natural rock formations created by the different rates of erosion of sandstone and gritstone. Rocks have been eroded into a variety of remarkable shapes, many of which have acquired descriptive names. There are four 'rocking stones', one of which, 'Idol Rock', rests on a pedestal of only 40cms and is estimated to weigh nearly 200 tonnes. This area of rough moorland enjoys splendid views over Nidderdale.*

**Carle Side/Beck/Moor:** * ON personal name, Karl. Karl's hillside/beck/moor.

**Cat Hole:** * OE catt/ON katt + OE/ON hol. The hollow where the wild cats live. See Catholes in the Dentdale section.

**Colsterdale:** Costerdale 1330. ME colster + ON dalr. The coal merchant's valley. (Coal was mined on Colsterdale Moor and a track leading off the moor is known as Coal Road).

**Coville House:**  Calfalhous 1308. OE calf + OE (ge) fall + OE hus. The 'house' in the woodland clearing where calves are kept.

**Dacre:**  Dacre 1086. The derivation is from a Celtic river-name based on the Welsh 'deigr', a teardrop. The trickling stream (cf Dacre near Ullswater).

**Darley:**  Derley 1388. OE deor + OE leah. The woodland clearing frequented by deer.

*Darley has two houses of special interest: Holme Hall with a steeply pitched thatched roof; and Low Hall, an Elizabethan manor house, the birthplace of Bishop Benson, Archbishop of Canterbury. Darley also had a corn mill on Darley Beck.*

**Dauber Gill:**  * Possibly ME dauber (a nickname) + ON gil. The plasterer's ravine.

**Dead Mans Hill:**  * The hill where dead men were found. (Three headless bodies were discovered buried in the peat here in 1728.)

**Duck Street:**  * Derivation obscure. It could be from the dialect 'duck', an abbreviation of 'duckstone', but without an early version of the name the etymology remains unexplained. The word 'street' refers to the ancient road leading from Fountains Abbey to the Abbey mines at Greenhow nearby. (Duck Street is a 1,400ft (425m) mountain).

**Flaystones:**  * This may be 'flagstones' (ON flaga), the large flat stones quarried in many locations in the Yorkshire Dales.

**Flout Hill:**  * Possibly from ON floi, a watery moss, or ON fljot, a stream.

**Fouldshaw:**  Foulschagh 1308. OE fugol + OE sceaga. The wood full of birdlife.

**Glasshouses:**  Glasshouses 1387. OE glaes + OE hus. The place where glass is made.

*This is a rare place-name reference to medieval English glass-making of which we have very few records. Glasshouses has left no record of its own glass-making industry but it did become the centre of a flax-spinning industry during the 19th century.*

**Gollinglith:**  * Derivation obscure. The first element might be the dialect word 'golling' meaning the catkins of the osier or willow; the second is probably ON hlith. The hill-slope where the osiers grow (by the River Burn).

**Gouthwaite:**  Gowthwaite 1598. ON personal name, Gaukr + ON thveit. Gaukr's clearing. (Gaukr also means the cuckoo; Gaukr could therefore be a nickname).

**Goyden Pot:**  * Derivation obscure: the second element may be OE denu and the first may be OE gota, a water-course. (At this pothole the River Nidd sinks underground to reappear further downstream).

**Greenhow:** Grenehow 1576. OE grene + ON haugr. The green hill.

*Lead was mined at Greenhow by the Romans who left behind two 'pigs' with Trajan inscriptions, and later by the Cistercians of Fountains Abbey who, in turn, were followed by modern industrial enterprises until the present century.*

**Guise Cliff:** Gisleclif 1142. ON personal name Gisli + OE clif. Gisli's cliff.

*This mile-long cliff is notable for its unusual rockshapes and crevices, many of which have been given names such as the Crocodile Rock and the Giant's Chair.*

**Hambleton Hill:** Hameldune 13th c. OE hamol + OE dun. The scarred hill.

**Hardcastle:** Hardcastell 1457. OE heard + OE castel. The bleak encampment or fort.

**Hartwith:** Hartwyth 1457. OE heorot + ON vithr. The wood frequented by harts.

**Haver Close:** * ON hafri + ME clos. The enclosure where oats are grown.

**Heathfield:** Higrefeld 1086. OE higera + OE feld. The open land frequented by magpies or jays.

*Heathfield is one of the few places in Upper Nidderdale to appear in the Domesday Book. Byland Abbey had a grange here. Lead mining has a long history in the vicinity with remaining evidence at Merryfield Beck.*

**Helks:** * OE helkn. The rough, stony field.

**Heyshaw:** Haghschag 1372. OE haga + OE sceaga. The wood in a hunting enclosure

**High Ruckles:** * There seems to be no early version of this name but it may refer to the dialect word 'ruckles', peat stacks. In Lucas's 'Nidderdale Studies' (1882) appears a reference to this: ....'they pile (the peats) into stacks which are called ruckles'.

**Hollin Hill:** * OE holegn + OE hyll. The hill covered with holly bushes.

**Hoodstorth:** Hudstorth 1793. ME personal name, Hude + ON storth. Hude's plantations.

**Ivin Waite:** * Possibly Dial 'ivin' = ivy + Dial 'waite' = a lookout. Ivy-covered look-out.

**Jenny Twig and her daughter Tib:** * These are two stone pillars standing isolated in the middle of desolate moorland. Their history is obscure.

**Keld Houses:** * ON kelda + ON hus. The houses by the spring.

**Kettlestang:** Ketellstang 1481. ON personal name, Ketil + ON stong. Ketil's pole. This marked the site of a cross on top of the hill.

**Kex Gill:** Kexegilbec 1226. Dial kex + ON gil. The ravine where teazels are found.

*Teazels were used in the cottage woollen industry for carding the wool and for raising the nap in the finishing process.*

**Kirkby Malzeard:** Kyrkeby-Malescard 1101. ON kirkju-by + OFr mal-assart. The place with the Church by the clearing with poor soil.

*Important in Norman times Kirkby Malzeard lost its castle long ago and in 1908 its Norman church was burned down. Only fragments remain but these include a beautiful doorway with typical Norman decorative motifs. There is some fine modern woodwork in the modern restoration. Kirkby Malzeard was part of the manorial holdings of the powerful Earl Gospatric, the pre-Conquest Earl of Northumberland.*

**Laverock Hall:** * OE lawerce + OE hall. The hall on the land where the larks nest.

**Leighton:** Lighton 1540. OE laec-tun. The herb or vegetable garden.

**Limley:** Lymlay 1379. OE lin + OE leah. The clearing where flax is grown.

**Lofthouse:** Lofthusum 1175. ON lopt-hus (husum = dative plural). The place by the houses with storage lofts or upper storeys.

**Low Laithe:** * ON lagr + ON hlatha. The lower barn. (See Brockabank Laithe p58)

**Masey Edge:** Mercy Edge 1609. The meaning of this name is unexplained.

**Masham:** Massan 1086/Masseham 1251. OE personal name, Maessa + OE ham. Maessa's homestead.

*Masham was an important manor both before and after the Norman Conquest. Like Kirkby Malzeard it was part of the lands of Gospatric, Earl of Northumberland. It was also a centre of the early Christian Church: numerous graves from Saxon and Viking times have been discovered here and the substantial shaft of a Saxon Cross still stands in the churchyard. Masham's great cobbled market place was the scene of the famous September fair held until early in the 20th century, one of the largest sheep fairs in the country and an occasion for much merrymaking. Masham is now better known as the home of Theakston's Breweries (open to the public on certain days)*

**Meugher:** Mukowe 1307. ON mjor + ON haugr. The small hill.

**Middlesmoor:** Middelsmor 1190. OE personal name, Midele + OE mor. Midele's moor.

*Middlesmoor is a pleasant hamlet, once a grange for Byland Abbey and, before that, most probably the site of a Saxon church. The present 19th century Church is dedicated to St. Chad and a Saxon Cross bearing the inscription 'Cross of St. Ceadda' is in the nave. Some of the best scenery in Nidderdale may be seen here.*

**Moscarr:** * ON mosi + ON kjarr. The marshy place covered in brushwood.

**Nabs:** * ON nabbi. A knoll or hillock.

**Noonstone:** * Probably a reference to a stone over which the sun stood at noon.

**Ouster Bank:** Ouslster Bank 1817. ON austr + ON erg. The hill pastures to the east.

**Owset Well:** * Probably Dial owse + ON sætr + OE wella. The spring at the seter where oxen pasture.

**Padside:** Padeside 1230. OE personal name, Pada + OE side. Pada's hill.

**Palley's Crags:** Pawlez Stanez 1540. OE palis + OE stan. The stones by the stakes or boundary fence. The boundary referred to was that between the lands of Fountains Abbey and those of the Forest of Knaresborough.

**Pateley Bridge:** Patleiagate 1175. OE paeth + OE leah. The forest clearing by the paths or tracks. The ON 'gata' is a superfluous addition. The paths referred to were those from Knaresborough and Ripon to Craven which crossed the River Nidd here by a ford. The first reference to a bridge is in 1320.

*Pateley Bridge was a small village until the arrival of the Scotsgate Quarries in the 19th century and the construction of the Bradford Corporation Reservoirs in the 20th century. The Incline, a gravity railway, transported the quarried flagstones to the main line and they were widely used in many public buildings including the National Gallery in London and also in Victoria Station. The reservoir work involved the building of the Nidderdale Light Railway with its station at Pateley Bridge to take men and materials up the valley to the Angram, Scar House and Gouthwaite Reservoirs. Of the older village there still remain the coaching inns, the 17th century sweet shop and apothecary's shop, St. Mary's church (ruins), the mill-race and the 18th century bridge. More modern buildings of interest are The Cocoa House, the Nidderdale Museum, St. Cuthbert's Church and The Playhouse. Pateley Bridge today is an attractive small town catering for walkers and tourists, and enhanced by its notable display of hanging baskets.*

**Pockstones:** Poxtonnes 1613. Dial pox-stone. The place with the pitted stones.

**Pott Hall:** The Hall near the rift in the limestone. ME potte: Yorkshire 'pot' as used here indicates not a pothole but a crevice in the limestone.

**Rainstang:** * ON rein + ON stong. A boundary post.

**Ramsgill:** Ramesgill 1198. ON personal name, Hrafn, or ON hramsa + ON gil.

Hrafn's ravine or the ravine where the wild garlic grows.

*Ramsgill is an attractive village at the head of Gouthwaite Reservoir which is now a nature reserve notable for its variety of bird species. A more dubious claim to fame is that Ramsgill was the birthplace of Eugene Aram, the murderer who disposed of his victim's body in St. Robert's Well at Knaresborough.*

**Raygill:** Ragill 1649. OE/ON ra + ON gil. Roebuck ravine.

**Redlish:** Radelez 1142. OE reod + OE lisc. The reedy marsh.

**Redshaw:** Redschate 1173. OE read + OE sceaga. The red wood.

**Ruscoe:** Ruscoe in Netherdale 1609. Possibly OE ruh + OE sceaga. The rough wood.

**Sigsworth:** Sixford 1184. ON personal name, Sikr + OE ford/ON vath. Sikr's ford.

**Skrikes Farm:** * Dial skrike/ON skraekja. The farm haunted by screech owls.

**Smelthouses:** A smelting mill was established here in the 14th century by the monks of Fountains Abbey to process the lead mined at Greenhow.

**Sowmire:** Surmire 1314. ON saurr + ON myrr. The sour marshland.

**Spittle Ings:** * OE spitel + ON eng. The meadows by the hospital. ('Hospital' often indicates a leper hospital founded by one of the religious Orders.)

**Stean:** Steane 1609. ON steinn. A stone. (Howstean is possibly ON hol + ON steinn: stony ravine.)

*Stean is best known for the Howstean Gorge where Howstean Beck flows through a limestone ravine with several accessible caves and fine scenery. A ticket is required to walk along the gorge, available from the cafe or the cottage nearby.*

**Steel Wood:** * OE stigel + OE sceaga. The wood with a stile.

**Stock Ridge:** * OE stocc + ON hryggr. The ridge covered with tree-stumps.

**Stott Fold:** * OE stod-fald. An enclosure for horses, a stud-fold.

**Summerbridge:** * Probably 'the bridge for use in summer'. Otherwise unexplained.

*Summerbridge became quite an industrial village in the 19th century with several mills and an iron foundry. Many of the vast iron fireplaces seen in Dales kitchens bear the name Joseph Todd who operated the foundry in the late 19th century.*

**Sype Land:** * Wet land. Dial sype = an area of wetland constantly oozing water.

**Tewit Farm:** * Peewit farm. Tewit is the northern name for the peewit or lapwing.

**Thornthwaite:**  Tornthueit 1230. OE/ON thorn + ON thveit. Thorn-tree clearing.

*Thornwood was widely used for baking: it gave the greatest heat. (See Psalm 58). Thornthwaite's early 19th century church is built on the site of a medieval chantry of St. Osyth. Thornthwaite has a true packhorse bridge over Darley Beck paved with flagstones and only 38 inches (95cms) wide.*

**Throstle Hill:**  Frostildehau 1142. ON personal name, Frosthildr + ON haugr. Frosthildr's hill.

**Thruscross:**  Thorecros 1142. ON personal name, Thorir + ON kros. Thorir's cross.

*Thruscross Mill is said to have been an appalling example of the cruel exploitation of child labour. A grave-pit nearby is alleged to be the burial place of the many children who died in the mill from overwork, harsh treatment and starvation.*

**Thorny Grane:**  * Probably OE thornig + ON grein. Thorny land near the river-fork. Two becks meet here, Steel House Gill and Thorny Grane Gill, to form the River Burn.

**Thrope:**  Trope 1198. ON thorp. An outlying farm or hamlet.

**Toft Gate:**  * ON topt + ON gata. An enclosure with a house or small farmstead lying near a path or cattle-track.

**River Washburn:**  Walkesburn 1130. OE personal name, Walc + OE burna. Walc's stream.

**Wath:**  Acchewath 1154. ODan personal name, Aki + ON vath. Aki's ford.

*Wath has a packhorse bridge (widened in 1890) across the River Nidd with a span of 51 feet. This replaced the ford. Both were probably important to give the farms over the river a route to the markets at Ripon and Kirkby Malzeard.*

**Wig Stones:**  * OE wigga + OE stan. Logan stones or rocking stones.

**Wilsill:**  Wifeles healh 1030. OE personal name, Wifele + OE halh. Wifele's nook of land.

*Wilsill was a village of hand-loom weavers in the 16th and 17th centuries and some of their long, cruck-framed cottages still remain. The trading links with the markets in Ripon are shown in the many footpaths and bridleways leading to the old Ripon road.*

**Woodale/Woogill:**  Woodaile 1594/Woogill 1861. OE woh + ON dalr/ON gil. The valley/ravine with a bend or crook. (cf Woodale in Wensleydale page 35).

**Yeadon:**  Iweden 1154. OE iw + OE denu. Yew-tree valley.

**Yorke's Folly:**  These two stone pillars built some 200 years ago by the local Yorke family are known as The Two Stoops. (ON stolpi = marker post).

## A

**a** ON a river
**abbat** OFr an abbot
**aecer** OE a plot of arable land
**aeppel** OE an apple
**aeppel-treow** OE an apple tree
**aers** OE arse
**aesc** OE an ash tree
**akr** ON a plot of arable land
**almr** ON an elm tree
**alor** OE an alder tree
**amore** OE a bunting (wild bird)
**anger** OE pasture land
**askr** ON an ash tree
**austr** ON east
**authr** ON desolate

## B

**baec-stan** OE a bake-stone
**balg** OE round (like a bulge)
**banke** OE a bank or hillside
**beam** OE a beam or a tree
**beinn** ON short
**bekkr** ON a beck or stream
**bel** OE a beacon

Skipton courtyard

**belle** OE bell-shaped
**beo** OE a bee
**beonet** OE bent-grass

**beorg** OE a hill or mountain
**berg** ON a hill or

mountain
**bere** OE barley
**berie** OE berry
**bigging** OE a building
**birki** ON a birch tree
**biscop** OE a bishop
**bjorr** ON a beaver
**bla/blar** ON dark or dark blue
**blaec** OE black or dark
**blaeingr** ON dark (often of water)
**blanda** ON to mix (often of liquids)
**bleikr** ON bleak, bare
**blesi** ON bare (of a hillside)
**bluber** ME bubbling springs
**boga** OE a curve (in a river or hillside)
**bor** OE a pointed headland
**borg** ON a fort
**borkr** ON the bark of a tree
**bothl-tun** OE an enclosure with buildings (a village)
**botm** OE the bottom (of a valley), a hollow
**brad** OE broad
**braec** OE a thicket
**brakni** ON bracken
**brand** ON a burned clearing
**brant** ON steep
**breithr** ON broad
**brende** OE a burned clearing
**brerig** OE covered in briars
**brocc-hol** OE a badger sett
**brom** OE broom
**brunnr** ON a stream, a

burn
**brycg/bryggja** OE/ON a bridge
**bucc** OE a buck
**bur** ON a storehouse
**burgaesn** OE a cairn or burial mound
**burh** OE a fort
**burh-tun** OE a fortified farmstead
**burna** OE a stream or burn
**bur-tre** OE an elder tree, a bortree
**buskr** ON a bush
**butte** ME a strip of land on the boundary
**by** ON a farmstead or hamlet
**byre** OE a byre or cowshed
**byjar-stathr** ON a place with a village (byjar = gen sing of by)

# C

**calf** OE a calf
**cam** OE the crest of a ridge
**castel** ME a castle or fort
**catt** OE a wild cat
**caul** Dial a dam or weir
**cautell** ME a fish-trap
**cetel** OE a bubbling stream (like a kettle)
**cirice** OE a church
**claepe** OE noisy (of a stream)
**clif** OE a cliff
**cloh** OE a ravine, a clough
**clos** ME an enclosed area, a close
**clud** OE a rock or mass of rock

**cluder** OE a mass of rocks or pile of rubble
**cnoll** OE a knoll or hilltop
**cocc** OE a woodcock
**cock-lake** OE a place where woodcock display
**colm** ME soot, coal dust
**colster** ME a coal merchant
**cosh** ME a hut
**cot** OE a cottage
**coupare** ME cooper
**coventree** Dial the guelder rose, a meeting-place
**craf** Br garlic
**crei** Wel fresh (water)
**crin** OIr dry (of a valley)
**croft** OE a small enclosure
**crumbaco** Br crooked
**cu** OE a cow
**cweorn** OE a quern
**cyln** OE a kiln
**cyning** OE the king

# D

**dael** OE a valley, a dale
**dalr** ON a valley, a dale
**dauber** ME a plasterer (a nickname)
**deigr** Wel a tear-drop
**denu** OE a valley, a dene
**deor** OE a deer
**derne** OE hidden
**dic** OE a rampart or embankment
**dile** OE dill
**dind** OIr a hill
**dodde** ME a round summit
**douky** Dial damp
**drum** Br a wooded ridge
**dub/dybb** OE a pool
**dufa** OE a dove

**dummock** Dial a dung heap
**dun** OE a hill
**dwfr** Wel water

# E

**earn** OE an eagle
**east** OE east
**eg/ey** OE/ON a water meadow
**eger** OE strong (of a river)
**eik** ON an oak tree
**eisa** ON to rush (of water)
**elri** ON an alder tree
**eng** ON a meadow
**epli** ON an apple tree
**erg** ON upland pastures
**eski** ON an ash tree
**estalon** OFr a stallion

# F

**fag** OE many-coloured
**fald** OE a fold
**(ge)fall** OE a woodland clearing
**fara** ON to go, to rush
**far-garthr** ON a sheepfold

**feld** OE open land, a field
**fit** ON a meadow by a river
**fjall** ON a mountain
**flaga** ON a flagstone
**flask** ON boggy ground
**flat** ON level ground
**flat** Dial a division of a common field
**fleke** Dial a hurdle or fence
**fleot** OE a stream
**fljot** ON a stream
**floi** ON a watery moss
**flosshe** ME a swamp
**fontein** OFr a spring
**ford** OE a ford
**fore** OE in front
**fors** ON a waterfall, a force
**fox** OE a fox
**fyrthe** OE wood(ed)

# G

**gaersing** OE pasture, grazing
**galga** OE gallows
**gapa** ON a chasm
**gara** OE a triangular piece of land

**garthr** ON an enclosure
**gata** ON a road
**gaukr** ON a cuckoo
**geat** OE a gate, an opening
**geil** ON a narrow valley
**gil** ON a ravine
**gingling** Dial rattling, jingling
**glaes** OE glass
**gnipa** ON a steep rocky place
**golling** Dial willow catkins (pussy-willow)
**gor** OE/ON covered in manure, dirty
**gota** OE a water-course
**graefe** OE a copse
**grar** ON grey
**great** OE large
**grein** ON a fork in a river or valley
**grene** OE green
**greot** OE gravel
**grima** OE a ghost or goblin
**gris** ON a young pig
**grjot** ON gravel
**(ge)haeg** OE an enclosure for hunting

Muker

85

# H

**haesel/hesli** OE/ON  hazel
**haeth** OE  heathland
**hafri** ON  oats
**haga** OE  an enclosure
**halh** OE  a nook of land
(e.g. in a river bend)
**halig** OE  holy, belonging
to the church
**hall** OE  a hall
**hals** ON  a pass through
the hills
**ham** OE  a homestead
**hamol** OE  a scarred
hillside
**har** OE  a tumulus, a heap
of stones
**haugr** ON  a hill
**heafod/hofuth** OE/ON  a
headland
**heah** OE  high
**heard** OE  hard to
cultivate
**hebble** Dial  a plank
bridge
**hegning** ON  enclosed
land
**helkn** OE  rough, stony
**hella** ON  a flat stone
**hellir** ON  a deep recess, a
cave
**helm** OE  a shelter, a hut,
the summit of a hill
**henn** OE  a bird
**heope** OE  the wild rose
**heorot** OE  a hart
**herde** OE  a shepherd
**herbergi** ON  an inn, a
shelter
**here-beorg** OE  an inn, a
shelter
**herkien** OE  to eavesdrop
**hestr** ON  a horse
**higera** OE  a jay, a magpie
**hind** OE  a hind
**hjortr** ON  a hart

**hlatha** ON  a barn
**hlaup** ON  a leap, 'a
fugitive'
**hlith** ON  a sloping
hillside
**hnaepp** OE  bowl-shaped
**hobbe** ME  a hobgoblin
**hol** OE/ON  a deep hollow
**holegn** OE  holly
**holmr** ON  a water-
meadow, an island
**hop** OE  a hanging valley
**hor** ON  high
**horu** OE  dirty, muddy
**hrafn** ON  a raven
**hramsa** ON  ramsons,
wild garlic
**hreod** OE  reedy
**hreysi** ON  a cairn
**hris** OE  brushwood
**hrutan(de)** OE  to roar,
roaring (of water)
**hufa** OE  a hood
**hus** OE/ON  a house, a
building (dative plural =
husum)
**hvammr** ON  a marshy
hollow
**hvarf** ON  a bend, a curve
**hvass** ON  pointed
**hverfr** ON  winding
**hvin** ON  gorse
**hvitr** ON  white
**hwit** OE  white
**hwaes** OE  pointed
**hyll** OE  a hill
**hyrcg** OE  a ridge
**hyrggr** ON  a ridge

# I

**ifig** OE  ivy
**ing-hyll** OE  a hilltop
**ing-tun** OE  a farmstead
belonging to ....
**ivin** Dial  ivy
**iw** OE  a yew tree

# K

**kal** ON  cabbage
**kaldr** ON  cold
**kambr** ON  the crest of a
ridge
**kapall** ON  a horse
**karl** ON  a freeman, a
yeoman
**katt** ON  a wild cat
**kelda** ON  a spring
**kerling** ON  an old
woman, a crone
**ketill** ON  a bubbling
spring (like a kettle)
**kex** Dial  a teazel
**kide** ME  a young goat
**kinn** ON  a sloping
hillside, a declivity
**kirkja** ON  a church
**kirkju-byr** ON  a place
with a church
**kith** ON  a young goat
**kjarr** ON  marsh covered
with brushwood
**klettr** ON  a steep cliff
**klint** ODan  a crag, a
rocky cliff
**knottr-ber** ON  the
knotberry or cloudberry
**knutr** ON  a rocky hillside
**kraka** ON  a crow
**kringla** ON  circular
**krokr** ON  a sharp bend
**kros** ON  a cross
**kunung** ON  a king
**kvi** ON  a fold (for cattle
or sheep)
**kyen** ME  cows (plural
form of OE cu)
**kyr** ON  a cow

# L

**lacu** OE  a stream
**laec-tun** OE  a herb or
vegetable garden

**lagr** ON low
**land** OE land, a strip of land in the common field
**lang/langr** OE/ON long
**launde** ME a forest glade
**lawerce** OE a lark
**leah** OE woodland clearing
**leikr** ON a place where animals or birds display
**lengan/lengja** OE/ON to linger, to rest
**lin** OE flax
**lisc** OE a marsh
**locere** Dial a shepherd
**lundr** ON a grove, a small wood
**lyng** ON heather

# M

**maed** OE a meadow
**maere** OE a boundary
**mal-assart** OFr a clearing with poor soil
**malr** ON a cove
**marr** ON a horse
**maurr** ON an ant
**mea** Dial a meadow, a pasture
**meisingr** ON a titmouse
**i melle** ME in the middle
**melr** ON a sandbank
**mere** OE a pool or lake
**mersc** OE a marsh
**methal** ON between, in the middle
**middel** OE middle
**mjor** ON small, narrow
**moel-fre** Wel a bare hill
**mor** OE a moor
**mos/mosi** OE/ON a bog, a moss
**mot** ON a meeting place (e.g. of rivers)
**muga** OE a heap of stones

**myln** OE a mill
**myrr** ON a bog, a marsh

# N

**nabbi** ON a knoll, a projecting point
**niwe** ON new
**nok** ME a nook of land
**north** OE/ON north

# O

**oter** OE an otter
**owse** Dial an ox
**oxa** OE an ox

# P

**paeth** OE a path
**palis** OE a fence, a palisade
**pas** ME a pass through the hills
**penn/penno** Wel/Br a hill
**piced** OE pointed
**pindere** ME a pinder
**pinn** OE a pinnacle, a pointed rock
**plat** ME a plot of land
**potte** ME a pothole or crevice
**pox-stone** Dial a pitted stone or rock
**praw** OE a look-out
**preost** OE a priest
**prien** ME to spy

# R

**ra** ON a roebuck
**rak/rake** ON/Dial a track to upland pastures
**rash** Dial a rocky patch in arable land
**rauthr** ON red
**raw** OE a row

**read** OE red
**rein** ON a boundary strip
**reod** OE reed
**rille** OE a brook or stream
**rith** OE a place by a stream
**riveling** ME a rivulet
**rotinn** ON rotten, soft
**ruckles** Dial peat stacks, hay cocks
**ruh** OE rough (of land)
**rum** ON cleared land, an open space
**ryth** ON a clearing
**rydding** OE cleared land, a clearing

# S

**sae/saer** OE/ON a lake
**saeti** ON a seat-shaped summit, a flat hilltop
**sætr** ON a seter, a summer farm in the uplands
**sand/sandr** OE/ON sand
**saurr** ON sour, muddy
**sceaga** OE a wood
**sceap** OE sheep
**sceot** OE a steep slope
**scraef** OE a hollow
**seaga** OE wetland, a marsh
**sel** ON a shieling
**selja** ON a willow tree
**seolfor** OE silver
**set-berg** ON a hill with a seat-shaped summit
**setl** OE a dwelling house
**shot** Dial a ewe in poor condition
**sic** OE a small stream, a water-meadow
**side** OE a hillside
**sjon** ON a look-out
**skali** ON a shieling
**skeppa** ON a beehive

**sker** ON a scar, a rocky outcrop
**skirr** ON bright, shining
**skjallr** ON resounding
**skogr** ON a wood
**skraekja/skrike** ON/OE a screech owl
**slaed** OE a valley
**slaeget** OE sheep pastures
**slakki** ON a hollow
**sleipr** ON slippery
**sletta** ON a level field
**smjor** ON butter
**sneis** ON covered in twigs
**sorell** OE sorrel
**sol** ON sun
**spital** ME a hospice or hospital
**staca** OE a stake
**stafn** ON a stake
**stakkr** ON a haystack
**stan/steinn** OE/ON a stone
**stede** OE the site (eg of a cowshed)
**stig/stigr** OE/ON a track, a path
**stigel** OE a stile, a path up a hill
**stirc** OE a stirk, a young ox
**stoc** OE an outlying farm
**stocc** OE a tree-stump
**stod-fald** OE a stud, an enclosure for horses
**stolpi** ON a marker post, a stoup
**stong** ON a pole (often a boundary marker)
**storth** ON a woodland plantation
**straet** OE a road
**strand** OE land at the water's edge, a beach
**stride** OE a narrow channel
**strother** OE a marshy area covered in brushwood

**stubbing** OE an area cleared of tree-stumps
**stumpr** ON a stump
**sumarr** ON summer
**sur** OE sour (soil)
**sutare/sutari** OE/ON a shoe-maker
**svatr** ON black, dark
**svirla** ON to swirl
**svithingr/svithinn** ON a clearing made by burning
**swaert** OE black, dark
**swilian** OE to swirl
**swin/svin** OE/ON swine
**sype** Dial wetland constantly oozing water

# T

**tack** Dial land hired out for cattle pasture
**tade** OE a toad
**tan/teinn** OE/Icel a boundary mark
**tatha/tathe** ON/Dial a home field spread with manure
**tewit** Dial a peewit
**thornig** OE thorny
**thorp** ON an outlying farm or hamlet
**threap** OE dispute
**thresc-feld** OE open space where threshing takes place
**thurs** ON a giant
**thruh** OE a drainage ditch
**thyrne** OE a thorn-bush
**topt** ON an enclosure with a house or building
**treow** OE a tree
**troll** ON a giant
**trun** OE circular
**tun** OE/ON a farm, a settlement
**turbarye** ME land where

turf is cut (for fuel)
**turf** OE turf
**tveit** ON thwaite, a clearing
**twisla** OE a river-fork, the land in such a fork

# U

**ule** OE an owl
**ulfr** ON a wolf

# V

**vath** ON a ford
**vatn** ON water
**vindr** ON wind
**vithr** ON a wood
**vra** ON a corner or nook of land

# W

**waegn** OE a wagon
**waite** Dial a look-out
**walh** OE a 'serf' - (referring to British displaced by Anglo-Saxon settlements)
**wella** OE a well or spring
**weorf** OE winding
**whamm** OE a marshy hollow
**wic** OE a farm
**wigga** OE a rocking stone, a logan stone
**wind** OE wind
**winter** OE winter
**withig** OE withy, willow, osier
**woh** OE crooked, with a bend
**wudu** OE a wood
**wulf** OE a wolf
**wyrt-tun** OE a herb or vegetable garden

Swaledale

## A

Abbotside We 23
Addingham Wh 65
Addleborough We 23
Agglethorpe We 24
Agill N 75
River Aire A 57
Airedale A 57
Airton A 58
Aisgill D 37
Aiskew S 13
Alum Pot R 47
Amerdale Dub Wh 65
Angram S 13

Angram N 75
Annaside S 13
Apedale We 24
Appersett We 24
Applegarth S 13
Appletreewick Wh 65
Apron full of Stones R 47
Arant Haw D 37
Arkengarthdale S 13
Arkleside We 24
Arkle Town S 13
Armathwaite N 75
Arnagill N 75
Arncliffe Wh 65
Arten Gill D 37

Ashfold Gill N 75
Askrigg We 24
Attermire R 47
Austwick R 47
Autherlands N 75
Aye Gill D 37
Aygill S 13
Aygill N 75
Aysgarth We 24

## B

Backstone Gill D 37
Backstone Gill N 75
River Bain We 24

Bainbridge We 24
Banger House N 75
Barben Beck Wh 65
Barbon D 38
Bardale We 25
Barden Wh 65
Bark House R 48
Barkin D 38
Batty Moss R 48
Baugh Fell D 38
Beamsley Wh 65
Bearsett We 25
Beckermonds Wh 66
Beecroft R 48
Beezleys R 48
Beldon S 13
Bell Busk A 58
Bents S 13
Bewerley N 75
Birkdale S 13
Birkrigg We 25
Birks D 38
Birkwith R 48
Birstwith N 76
Bishopdale We 23
Bishopside N 76
Blades D 38
Blakamaya R 48
Blakethwaite S 13
Blands D 38
Blayshaw N 76
Blazefield N 76
Blea Moor R 48
Blean We 25
Blubberhouses N 76
Boggart's Roaring Holes R 48
Bolton Abbey Wh 66
Booze S 13
Bordley A 58
Borrett D 38
Borrins R 48
Borwins We 25
Bouthwaite N 76
Brackenbottom R 48
Braida Garth R 48
Braidley We 25
Braithwaite We 25
Braithwaite N 76
Bramaskew D 38

Brandrith N 76
Brandstone Beck N 76
Brant Fell D 38
Branthwaite D 38
Brass Castle Wh 66
Breaks Fold N 76
Brearlands Wh 66
Brigflatts D 38
Brimham N 76
Brimham Rocks N 76
Broadrake R 48
Brockabank Laithe A 58
Brockholes Gill D 38
Brough Hill We 25
Bruntscar R 48
Buckden Wh 66
Burnsall Wh 66
Burtersett We 25
West Burton We 26
Buttertubs S 13

# C

Caldbergh We 26
The Calf D 38
Calton A 58
Cam R 48
Capon Hall A 58
Capplestones Wh 67
Carle Side N 76
Carlin Gill D 39
Carlton-in-Coverdale We 26
Carperby We 26
Carrs R 49
Castleberg R 49
Castle Bolton We 26
Castle Dykes We 27
Castle Haw D 38
Castley D 39
Cat Hole N 76
Cat Holes D 39
Catrigg Force R 49
Cautley D 39
CB S 14
Chapel-le-Dale R 49
Clapdale R 49
Clapham R 49
Cleasby S 14
Cleatop R 49

Clint D 39
River Clough D 39
Clowder Wh 67
Cocklake Side We 27
Cogden S 14
Cogill We 27
Coleby We 27
Colsterdale N 76
Combe Scar R 49
Conistone Wh 67
Copperthwaite S 14
Cosh Wh 67
Cotescue We 27
Cotterdale We 27
Countersett We 27
Coventree D 39
River Cover We 27
Coverdale We 23
Coverham We 27
Coville House N 77
Cowgill D 39
Cowper Cote A 58
Cowper Gill D 39
Cracoe Wh 67
Crake Moor A 59
Crackpot S 14
Craven A 59
Cray Wh 67
Crina Bottom R 49
Cringley Hill S 14
Crook of Lune D 39
Crookrise A 59
Crummackdale R 50
Cubeck We 28

# D

Dacre N 77
Dandry Garth D 39
Dandry Mire D 39
Danny Bridge D 40
Darley N 77
Darnbrook A 59
Dauber Gill N 77
Dead Man's Hill N 77
River Dee D 40
Deerstones Wh 67
Dent D 40
Dentdale D 36

Devil's Apronful  Wh  67
River Dibb  Wh  67
Dibble's Bridge  Wh  67
Dillicar  D  40
Dodd Fell  We  28
River Doe  R  50
Douk Caves  R  50
Douky Bottom Cave  Wh  67
Dowbiggin  D  40
Downholme  S  14
Drebley  Wh  67
Drumaldrace  We  28
Duck Street  N  77
Dummacks  D  40

# E

Eastby  A  59
Ecker Secker Gill  D  40
Elbolton  Wh  67
Eller Beck  R  50
Eller Beck  Wh  67
Ellerton  S  14
Embsay  A  59
Eshber  Wh  67
Eshton  A  59
Eskeleth  S  14

# F

Faggergill  S  14
Fawcett  D  40
Fawes  D  40
Feetham  S  15
Feizor  R  50
Firbank  D  40
Flamstone Pinn  We  28
Flasby  A  59
Flask  Wh  67
Flaystones  N  77
The Fleak  S  15
Fleensop  We  28
Fleets  Wh  67
Floshes Hill  We  28
Flout Hill  N  77
Flust  D  41
Foredale  R  50
Fornah Gill  A  59
Fossdale  We  28

Fouldshaw  N  77
Fountains Fell  A  59
Foxup  Wh  67
Fremington  S  15
Frostrow  D  41

# G

Gammersgill  We  28
Gaping Gill  R  50
Gargrave  A  60
Garrellgum  Wh  67
Garsdale  D  37
Gastack  D  41
Gauber  R  50
Gawthrop  D  41
Gayle  We  28
Gearstones  R  50
Ghaistrill's Strid  Wh  68
Giggleswick  R  50
Glasshouses  N  77
Gollinglith  N  77
Gordale  A  60
Gouthwaite  N  77
Goyden Pot  N  77
Gragareth  R  51
Grassington  Wh  68
Great Close  A  60
Greenhow  N  78
Greets  S  15
Grimwith  Wh  68
Grinton  S  15
Grisedale  D  41
Guise Cliff  N  78
Gunner Fleet  R  51
Gunnerside  S  15

# H

Hacker Gill  D  41
Halton East  Wh  68
Halton Gill  Wh  68
Hambleton Hill  N  78
Hanlith  A  60
Harber  R  51
Harbour Gill  D  41
Hardcastle  N  78
Hardraw  We  28
Harkerside  S  16

Harland  We  28
Harmby  We  29
Hartlakes  S  16
Hartlington  Wh  68
Hartwith  N  78
Haver Close  N  78
Haverdale  S  16
Hawes  We  29
Hawkswick  Wh  68
Haws House  R  51
Healaugh  S  16
Heathfield  N  78
Hebblethwaite  D  41
Hebden  Wh  68
Helks  N  78
Hell Gill  D/We  41
Hell Gill Beck  D/We  41
Hellifield  R  51
Helm  We  29
Helmside  D  41
Helwith  S  16
Helwith Bridge  R  51
Henstone Band  Wh  68
Hesleden  Wh  68
Hestholme  We  29
Hetton  A  60
Hewthwaite  D  41
Heyshaw  N  78
High Ruckles  N  78
Hindlethwaite  We  29
Hining  D  41
Hobdale Beck  D  41
Hollin Hill  N  78
Hollins  D  41
Holly Platt  R  51
Hoodstorth  N  78
Hoove  S  16
Horrabank  We  29
Horse House  We  29
Horton-in-Ribblesdale  R  51
Howgill Fells  D  42
Hubberholme  Wh  68
Hudswell  S  16
Hull Pot  R  52

# I

Ilkley  Wh  69
Ingleborough  R  52
Ingle Bridge  A  60

91

Ingleton  R  52
Ingmire  D  42
Ingsque  S  16
Ivelet  S  16
Ivescar  R  52
Ivin Waite  N  78

# J

Jenny Twig and her
daughter Tib  N  78
Jervaulx  We  29
Jingling Pot  R  52

# K

Kail Hill  Wh  69
Keld  S  16
Keld Houses  N  78
Kettlestang  N  78
Kettlewell  Wh  69
Kex Gill  N  78
Kidhaw Gate  Wh  70
Kidstones  We  30
Kilnsey  Wh  70
Kingsdale  R  46
Kirkby Malham  A  60
Kirkby Malzeard  N  79
Kirk Gill  Wh  70
Kisdon  S  16
Kitley Hill  S  17
Knipe Scar  Wh  70
Knoutberry Haw  D  42
Knowe Fell  A  60
Knudmaning  D  42

# L

Lainger House  Wh  70
Lamps Moss  D  42
Langbar  Wh  70
Langcliffe  R  52
Langstrothdale  Wh  64
Langthwaite  S  17
Laund  Wh  70
Laverock Hall  N  79
Lea Yeat  D  42
Leighton  N  79

Lenacre  We  30
Leyburn  We  30
Limley  N  79
Ling Gill  R  52
Linton  Wh  70
Litherskew  We  30
Litton  Wh  71
Littondale  Wh  64
Locker Tarn  We  30
Lofthouse  N  79
Long Preston  R  53
Lops Wath  S  17
Low Laithe  N  79
Low Row  S  17
Lunds  D  42
River Lune  R  52

# M

Maiden Castle  S  17
Malham  A  60
Malhamdale  A  57
Mallerstang  D  42
Marrick  S  17
Marsett  We  30
Marske  S  17
Marthwaite  D  43
Masey Edge  N  79
Masham  N  79
Masongill  R  53
Mastiles  A  61
Mearbeck  R  53
Melbecks Moor  S  17
Melmerby  We  30
Meughar  N  79
Middleham  We  30
Middlesmoor  N  79
Millthrop  D  43
Mosscar  N  80
Mossdale  We  31
Moughton  R  53
Muker  S  17

# N

Nabs  N  80
Nappa  We  31
Naughtberry Hill  We  31

Neals Ing  R  53
Needle House  D  43
Newbiggin  We  31
Newby Head  R  53
River Nidd  74
Nidderdale  N  74
Nine Standards  S  18
Noonstone  N  80
Norber  R  53
Nussey House  Wh  71

# O

Old Cote  Wh  71
Orms Gill  A  61
Otterburn  A  61
Oughtershaw  Wh  71
Ouster Bank  N  80
Outhgill  D  43
Owset Well  N  80
Oxenber  R  53
Oxnop  S  18
Oxque  S  18

# P

Pace Gate  Wh  71
Padside  N  80
Palley's Crags  N  80
Parcevall Hall  Wh  71
Pateley Bridge  N  80
Pecca Falls  R  53
Penhill  We  31
Penyghent  R  53
Pikedaw  A  61
Pinder Stile  Wh  71
Platt  D  43
Pockstones  N  80
Posforth Gill  Wh  71
Pott Hall  N  80
Preston-under-Scar  We  31
Pry Hill  S  18
Punchard  S  18

# R

Rainscar  Wh  71
Raisgill  Wh  71

Rainstang  N  80
Rampsholme  S  18
Ramsgill  N  80
Ranelands  Wh  71
Rash  D  43
Rathmell  R  53
Ravenseat  S  18
Rawridding  D  43
River Rawthey  D  43
Raydale  We  31
Raygill  D  43
Raygill  N  81
Rayside  R  53
Redlish  N  81
Redmire  We  31
Redshaw  N  81
Reeth  S  18
River Ribble  R  46
Ribblesdale  R  46
Richmond  S  19
Riddings  S  20
Riddings  D  43
Rise Hill  D  43
Rivling  D  43
Rottenbutts  D  43
Routen Gill  We  31
Rowten Pot  R  54
Ruecrofts  D  43
Ruscoe  N  81
Rylestone  Wh  71

# S

Sannat Hall  R  54
Sarthwaite  D  43
Satron  S  20
Scaleber  R  54
Scales  D  43
Scales  R  54
Scoska  Wh  71
Scosthrop  A  61
Scotchergill  D  43
Scrafton  We  31
Seata  We  31
Sedbergh  D  44
Sedbusk  We  31
Sell Gill  R  54
Selside  R  54
Semer Water  We  32

Settle  R  54
Settlebeck  D  44
Shot Lathe  S  20
Shunner Fell  S  20
Sigsworth  N  81
Silverdale  R  54
Simonstone  We  32
Skeb Sceugh  S  20
Skell Gill  We  32
Skipton  A  61
Skir Beck  R  54
River Skirfare  Wh  71
Skirethorns  Wh  72
Skirwith  R  54
Skrikes Farm  N  81
Skyreholme  Wh  72
Skythorns  Wh  72
Slack  D  44
Slapestones Wath  We  32
Sleddale  We  32
Sleets  A  62
Sleights  R  54
Smarber  S  20
Smearsett  R  54
Smelthouses  N  81
Smorthwaite  D  44
Snaizeholme  We  32
Sorrelskyes  We  32
Sour Nook  S  20
Southerscales  R  54
Sowerthwaite  R  54
Sowmire  N  81
Spennithorne  We  32
Spice Gill  D  44
Spittle Croft  Wh  72
Spittle Ings  N  80
Stackhouse  R  54
Stainforth  R  54
Stake Moss  We  32
Stalling Busk  We  32
Stang  S  20
Starbotton  Wh  72
Stean  N  81
Steel Wood  N  81
Stirton  A  62
Stockdale  R  55
Stock Ridge  N  81
Stolerston  S  20
Stonesdale  S  20

Stony Raise  We  32
Storiths  Wh  72
Storrs  R  55
Storthwaite  S  20
Stott Fold  N  81
Strans  Wh  72
The Strid  Wh  72
Stubbing  S  20
Studfold  R  55
Stump Cross  Wh  72
Sulber  R  55
Summerbridge  N  81
Summerscales  Wh  72
River Swale  S  12
Swaledale  S  12
Swarth Greaves  D  44
Swarth Moor  R  55
Swinacote  We  33
Swineside  We  33
Swinithwaite  We  33
Sype Land  N  81

# T

Taitlands  R  55
Tan Hill  S  20
Taythes  D  44
Tewit Farm  N  81
Thiernswood  S  20
Thoralby  We  33
Thoragill  A  62
Thoresby  We  33
Thorlby  A  62
Thornthwaite  N  82
Thornton Force  R  55
Thornton-in-Lonsdale  R  55
Thornton Rust  We  33
Thorny Grane  N  82
Thorough Mea  D  44
Thorpe  Wh  72
Threapland  Wh  72
Threshfield  Wh  72
Thrope  N  82
Throstle Hill  N  82
Thruscross  N  82
Thursgill  D  44
Thwaite  S  21
Thwaite  D  44
Toft Gate  N  82

Tofts  D  44
Trenhouse  A  62
Trollers Gill  Wh  73
Trow Gill  R  55
Trunla Gill  Wh  73
Turbary Pasture  R  55
Turf Moor Hush  S  21
River Twiss  R  56
Twistleton  R  56

# U

Uldale  D  44
Ulfers Gill  We  33
Ulshaw  We  33
River Ure  We  33

# W

Wainwath  We  33
Walden  We  33
River Washburn  N  82
Wasset Fell  We  34

Wath  N  82
Watlowes  A  62
Wegber  We  34
Wensley  We  34
Wensleydale  We  22
West Burton  We  26
Wham  S  21
Wham  D  45
Wham  R  56
The Whams  Wh  73
Wharfe  R  56
River Wharfe  Wh  63
Wharfedale  Wh  63
Whaw  S  21
Whernside  R  56
Whinhaugh  Wh  73
Whins  D  45
Whitaside  S  21
Whitsundale  S  21
Widdale  We  34
Wig Stones  N  82
Wilsill  N  82

Winder  D  45
Windleside  Wh  73
Winshaw  R  56
Winskill  R  56
Winterburn  A  62
Winterings  S  21
Winterscales  R  56
Witton (East/West)  We  34
Woodale  We  35
Woodale  N  82
Woogill  N  82
Worton  We  35

# Y

Yarnbury  Wh  73
Yeadon  N  82
Yockenthwaite  Wh  73
Yordas Cave  R  56
Yoredale  We  35
Yorescott  We  35
Yorke's Folly  N  82

Reeth

# BIBLIOGRAPHY

**A short selection from the many books written on the Yorkshire Dales:**
D. Brumhead  Geology explained in the Yorkshire Dales and on the Yorkshire Coast (David & Charles 1979)
R. Fieldhouse & B. Jennings  A History of Richmond and Swaledale (Phillimore 1978)
J. & E. Forder  Open Fell, Hidden Dale (b/w photography) (F. Peters 1985)
M. Hartley & J. Ingilby  Life and Tradition in the Yorkshire Dales (Dalesman 1985)
N. Pevsner  The Buildings of England: The North Riding (Penguin 1968)
N. Pevsner  The Buildings of England: The West Riding (Penguin 1968)
A. Raistrick  The Yorkshire Dales (Dalesman 1991)
A. Raistrick  Malham and Malham Moor (Dalesman 1983)
A. Raistrick  Buildings of the Yorkshire Dales (Dalesman 1976)
C. Speakman  Complete Dales Walker: Vol 2 - The Southern Dales  (Dalesman 1994)
A. Wainwright  Walks in Limestone Country (Westmorland Gazette 1970)
T. Waltham  Yorkshire Dales: Limestone Country (Constable 1987)
T. Waltham  Official Guide to the Yorkshire Dales National Park (1987)
G. White  The Complete Dales Walker: Vol. 1 - The Northern Dales (Dalesman 1994)
G. N. Wright  Roads and Trackways in the Yorkshire Dales (Moorland 1985)
G. N. Wright  The Yorkshire Dales (David & Charles 1986)

**Place-name reference books:**
K. Cameron  English Place-names (Batsford 1961)
E. Ekwall  Concise Dictionary of English Place-names (OUP 1960)
E. Ekwall  English River-names (OUP 1928)
R. Gambles  Lake District Place-names (Dalesman 1994)
P. Metcalfe  Place-names of the Yorkshire Dales (North Yorks Marketing 1992)
D. Mills  Place-names of Lancashire (Batsford 1976)
A. H. Smith  English Place-name Elements: 2 Vols. (CUP 1956)
A H. Smith  Place-names of the North Riding (CUP 1928)
A. H. Smith  Place-names of the West Riding: Parts 6 & 7 (CUP 1961)
J. Wright  The English Dialect Dictionary (Frowde 1898)

**Other books by the author:**
Man in Lakeland
Place-names of the Lake District
Out of the Forest: The Natural World and the Place-names of Cumbria
The Spa Resorts and Mineral Springs of Cumbria
Walks on the Borders of Lakeland